Desegregating Ourselves

Dedication

I dedicate this book to all the adults who are seeking to desegregate their lives in order to be cross-cultural for themselves and create school environments that humanize the lived experiences of populations who experience marginalization!

Desegregating Ourselves

Challenging the Biases That Perpetuate Inequities in Our Schools

Edward Fergus

CORWIN
A Sage Company

FOR INFORMATION:

Corwin

A SAGE Company

2455 Teller Road

Thousand Oaks, California 91320

(800) 233-9936

www.corwin.com

SAGE Publications Ltd.

1 Oliver's Yard

55 City Road

London EC1Y 1SP

United Kingdom

SAGE Publications India Pvt. Ltd.

Unit No 323-333, Third Floor, F-Block

International Trade Tower Nehru Place

New Delhi 110 019

India

SAGE Publications Asia-Pacific Pte. Ltd.

18 Cross Street #10-10/11/12

China Square Central

Singapore 048423

Vice President and
  Editorial Director: Monica Eckman
Senior Publisher: Jessica Allan
Senior Acquisitions Editor: Megan Bedell
Senior Content
  Development Editor: Mia Rodriguez
Content Development
  Manager: Lucas Schleicher
Senior Editorial Assistant: Natalie Delpino
Project Editor: Amy Schroller
Copy Editor: Melinda Masson
Typesetter: C&M Digitals (P) Ltd.
Cover Designer: Candice Harman
Marketing Manager: Melissa Duclos

Copyright © 2024 by Corwin Press, Inc.

All rights reserved. Except as permitted by U.S. copyright law, no part of this work may be reproduced or distributed in any form or by any means, or stored in a database or retrieval system, without permission in writing from the publisher.

When forms and sample documents appearing in this work are intended for reproduction, they will be marked as such. Reproduction of their use is authorized for educational use by educators, local school sites, and/or noncommercial or nonprofit entities that have purchased the book.

All third-party trademarks referenced or depicted herein are included solely for the purpose of illustration and are the property of their respective owners. Reference to these trademarks in no way indicates any relationship with, or endorsement by, the trademark owner.

Printed in the United States of America

Library of Congress Cataloging-in-Publication Data

Names: Fergus, Edward, 1974- author.

Title: Desegregating ourselves : challenging the biases that perpetuate inequities in our schools / Edward Fergus.

Description: Thousand Oaks, California : Corwin, [2024] | Includes bibliographical references and index.

Identifiers: LCCN 2023057620 | ISBN 9781071888872 (paperback : acid-free paper) | ISBN 9781071888919 (epub) | ISBN 9781071888902 (epub) | ISBN 9781071888896 (pdf)

Subjects: LCSH: Racism in education—United States. | White supremacy (Social structure)—United States—History. | Segregation in education—United States. | School integration—United States. | Intelligence levels—Social aspects—United States. | Poverty—United States.

Classification: LCC LC212.52 .F467 2024 | DDC 371.829/00973—dc23/eng/20240316

LC record available at https://lccn.loc.gov/2023057620

This book is printed on acid-free paper.

SUSTAINABLE FORESTRY INITIATIVE   Certified Sourcing
www.forests.org
SFI-00756

24 25 26 27 28 10 9 8 7 6 5 4 3 2 1

DISCLAIMER: This book may direct you to access third-party content via Web links, QR codes, or other scannable technologies, which are provided for your reference by the author(s). Corwin makes no guarantee that such third-party content will be available for your use and encourages you to review the terms and conditions of such third-party content. Corwin takes no responsibility and assumes no liability for your use of any third-party content, nor does Corwin approve, sponsor, endorse, verify, or certify such third-party content.

Contents

Contents of Companion Website	vii
Acknowledgments	ix
About the Author	xi

Introduction — 1

Chapter 1: History of Using Whiteness to Create Ethno-Racial Segregation — 21

Chapter 2: Fear of Losing the Standard: From 20th Century Desegregation to 21st Century Anti-Integration — 47

Chapter 3: Colorblindness Belief: Ignoring Race as a Strategy for Maintaining Social Desirability — 67

Chapter 4: Deficit Thinking and Poverty Disciplining: Our Societal Fixation on Poverty — 91

Chapter 5: Interrupting Bias-Based Beliefs Built on Whiteness — 115

Appendices

Appendix 1: Reflecting on Our Whiteness Exposure	128
Appendix 2: Shopping Cart List of Experiences: Everyday Colorblindness and Evasiveness	130
Appendix 3: Colorblindness Reflection Activity	132
Appendix 4: Shopping Cart List of Experiences: Everyday Deficit Thinking and Poverty Disciplining	134
Appendix 5: Deficit Thinking and Poverty Disciplining Reflection Activity	136
Appendix 6: Exploring Our Current Cross-Cultural Lives, Skills, and Competencies	138
Appendix 7: Additional Cross-Cultural Activities	140
Appendix 8: Professional Development Template for Equity Belief Work: School Equity Team Tool	144

References   149

Index   157

Contents of Companion Website

Appendix 1: Reflecting on Our Whiteness Exposure

Appendix 2: Shopping Cart List of Experiences: Everyday Colorblindness and Evasiveness

Appendix 3: Colorblindness Reflection Activity

Appendix 4: Shopping Cart List of Experiences: Everyday Deficit Thinking and Poverty Disciplining

Appendix 5: Deficit Thinking and Poverty Disciplining Reflection Activity

Appendix 6: Exploring Our Current Cross-Cultural Lives, Skills, and Competencies

Appendix 8: Professional Development Template for Equity Belief Work

Please visit the companion website for downloadable resources at
resources.corwin.com/FergusDesegregating

Acknowledgments

The concept of this book emerged many years ago in graduate school. Upon reading an article about identity construction I stumbled onto the idea that each person travels their social lives filling a shopping cart with all sorts of experiences. My enduring concern—one that continues to center the way I live my life—is how to make sense of and interrupt the experiences in our shopping carts that keep us segregated by race, ethnicity, language, sexuality, gender, and religion.

Writing a book is always an amazing journey. This book gave me an opportunity to get input from my family, specifically my youngest son, Sean. I greatly appreciate Sean for his amazing support and changing my shopping cart, and Javier for teaching me fatherhood. I also need to thank the unrelenting champion of my career, Lorelei Vargas; thank you for allowing me to evolve. My other family includes my amazing friends. Each of you has the amazing, uncanny ability to care for others, to be unapologetic about your wonderful personality, and to share your brilliance with others. Thank you for being such an important family of friends!

I am also thankful for the many school district staff who I met over these 15 years; thank you for being such an inspiration and showcasing how practitioners take up the mantle of equity!

About the Author

Edward (Eddie) Fergus is a professor of urban education in the School of Arts and Sciences at Rutgers University–Newark. Prior to joining Rutgers University–Newark, Dr. Fergus was an associate professor of urban education and policy at Temple University (2017–2022), assistant professor of educational leadership and policy at New York University (2013–2017), and deputy director of the Metropolitan Center for Urban Education at New York University (2004–2013). As a former high school social studies teacher, program evaluator, and community school program director, Dr. Fergus is continuously approaching research with attention to its application within educational settings. Dr. Fergus's work is on the intersection of educational policy and outcomes with a specific focus on Black and Latino boys' academic and social engagement outcomes, disproportionality in special education and suspensions, and school climate conditions. He has published more than four dozen articles, book chapters, and evaluation reports and five books: *Skin Color and Identity Formation: Perceptions of Opportunity and Academic Orientation Among Mexican and Puerto Rican Youth* (author, Routledge Press, 2004), *Invisible No More: Disenfranchisement of Latino Men and Boys* (co-editor, Routledge Press, 2011), *Schooling for Resilience: Improving Trajectory of Black and Latino Boys* (co-author, Harvard Education Press, 2014), *Solving Disproportionality and Achieving Equity* (author, Corwin, 2016), and

Boyhood and Masculinity Construction in the US (co-editor, Routledge Press, forthcoming). Dr. Fergus has worked with over 120 school districts since 2004 on educational equity and school reform, specifically addressing disproportionality in special education and suspension. He also partners with state education departments and serves on various boards, such as the New York State Juvenile Justice Advisory Group (2010–present), Yonkers Public Schools Board of Education (2011–2013 and 2019–2021), and National Center for Learning Disabilities (2020–present), and is an expert consultant for the U.S. Department of Justice Civil Rights Division Educational Opportunities Section (2014–2016), New York State Attorney General's Office (2022), and NAACP Legal Defense Fund (2018).

Dr. Fergus received a bachelor's degree in political science and secondary education (broad field social studies) from Beloit College and a doctorate in educational policy and social foundations from the University of Michigan.

Introduction

Filling Our Shopping Carts With Segregated Life Experiences

Modern science has revealed that all human beings are 99.9% alike in their genetic makeup. We differ, however, in our lived experiences. Our beliefs, attitudes, and opinions are largely informed by an accumulation of life experiences, and our lived experiences are, to some degree, influenced by the history that preceded our birth.

In 1965, the acclaimed author James Baldwin reminded us that *the great force of history comes from the fact that we carry it within us* (Grossman, 2016). Americans descended from enslaved African people must live with this reality every day. The legacy of their ancestors' enslavement, a period that began in the early 1600s, lives on in our legal system and our schools. Enslaved persons were denied access to reading and writing over the course of generations—a denial legally sanctioned through slave codes. While such restrictions were intended to ensure the sustainability of the slave trade, the justification was rooted in assumptions about the inherent superiority of White males, and White families played a functional role in sustaining such assumptions. In *Raising Racists: The Socialization of White Children in the Jim Crow South*, Kristina DuRocher (2011) documents the racialization White children experienced that they similarly carried forward:

> White southern parents' instruction in regulating relations between the races was grounded in a highly idealized and nostalgic vision of a paternalistic white society. The ideological objective of this instruction, however unrealistic, was that the New South should replicate the romanticized social order of slavery. (p. 14)

DuRocher goes further to outline how parents received advice guides on raising children, particularly from faith-based institutions, that professed, in particular, that White girls shall remain pure in order to maintain the racial privilege:

> Southern advice guides underscored that parents' foremost duty was to teach their children their social roles, including appropriate gender roles. The 1935 manual *Preparing for Parenthood*, published in Florida, required that a proper home include "both Father as Protector, and Mother, as caretaker and trainer" . . . Due to this threat, authors of advice books emphasized the parents' duty to teach morality, especially to white girls, upon whose shoulders the future of white domination rest. (pp. 16–17)

While White children were taught to maintain their racial privilege long after the Emancipation Proclamation, Black Americans continued to be denied the same educational opportunities as their White counterparts under the law of the land. The Supreme Court's 1896 *Plessy v. Ferguson* decision established the separate but equal doctrine that placed Black children in segregated schools for over 50 years. Segregation was an enactment of the race-based assumption that Whites are superior and Blacks are inferior—the same assumption used to justify slavery. The *Plessy* case involved the Citizens' Committee comprised of Black men challenging a Louisiana state law that required separate train cars based on race. The Supreme Court's majority opinion upheld the constitutionality of the law and utilized notions of White superiority as its rationale: "If one race be inferior to the other socially, the Constitution of the United States cannot put them upon the same plane."[1] This ruling was not challenged until 1951, when *Brown v. Board of Education* was tried initially in Kansas courts. In fact, the detrimental effects of a racist ideology were only recognized after a successful legal campaign against it. Walter A. Huxman, one of three judges in the Kansas Supreme Court, stated in his opinion that legalized segregation resulted in an inferiority complex among Black children:

> Segregation of white and colored children in public schools has a detrimental effect upon the colored children. The impact is greater when it has the sanction of law; for the policy of separating the races is usually interpreted as denoting the

---

[1] U.S. National Archives and Records Administration. (2022, February 8). *Milestone documents:* Plessy v. Ferguson *(1896)*. https://www.archives.gov/milestone-documents/plessy-v-ferguson

inferiority of the negro group. A sense of inferiority affects the motivation of a child to learn. Segregation with the sanction of law, therefore, has a tendency to retard the educational and mental development of negro children and to deprive them of some of the benefits they would receive in a racial integrated school system.[2]

Judge Huxman's language couldn't be more explicit. The words *the policy of separating the races is usually interpreted as denoting the inferiority of the negro group* are an open acknowledgment of the deficit-based ideology that had been an operational feature of our education system, while White children explicitly and quietly absorbed in school and at home their cultural experiences as the norm and superior. Moreover, the claim that such practices have a detrimental effect on Black children encouraged further legal pursuits by the National Association for the Advancement of Colored People (NAACP) to challenge school segregation by showcasing its adverse effects. As a result of the eventual *Brown* decision in 1954, the Supreme Court provided an approach toward educational equity built on at least two pillars: (1) equal access to school facilities and educational practices such as curriculum and high-quality teachers, and (2) social, curricular, and instructional strategies that interrupt bias-based beliefs and elevate the humanity of marginalized populations. The primary work of our school systems over the last 70 years has focused on meeting the objectives of the first pillar in the form of technical solutions such as enrollment integration and bussing policies. The second pillar, which necessitates nothing less than critically examining and disrupting the deficit-based biases and belief systems that undergird our education policies and practices, is less frequently addressed. The intent of this book is to guide K–12 professionals in enacting the second pillar of *Brown*, beginning with interrogating the ideology of Whiteness. Before engaging the rest of the chapters, you must first understand the concept of Whiteness and its maintenance of disproportionality. Then understand how we all absorb Whiteness in our everyday experiences of bias.

What Is Whiteness?

Throughout this book, I use the term *Whiteness* to signify a specific ideology. I also use the term *White*, which is not synonymous with *Whiteness*. In fact, these frequently misunderstood and conflated

---

[2]Linder, D. O. (2023). *Famous trials:* Brown et al. v Board of Education of Topeka, Shawnee County, Kansas et al. UMKC. https://www.famous-trials.com/brownvtopeka/658-brownhuxman

terms connote very different ideas. When I reference *White*, I am using a nation-state definition of belonging to that racial group. According to the U.S. Census Bureau, *White* describes

> a person having origins in any of the original peoples of Europe, the Middle East, or North Africa. It includes people who indicate their race as "White" or report responses such as German, Irish, English, Italian, Lebanese, and Egyptian. The category also includes groups such as Polish, French, Iranian, Slavic, Cajun, Chaldean, etc.[3]

This definition hints at another important distinction. Among those who identify as White are separate categories of ethnic identification. The term *ethno-racial* entails both ethnic and racial classification (Fergus, 2004). Among Whites, common ethnic identifications include Italian American, Polish American, Jewish American, and so on. These identification tools reflect the contours existing within the White identity. The title of a popular book, *How the Irish Became White* (Ignatiev, 2009), reveals an important historical truth: Each European immigrant group had to earn the distinction of a White identity through acculturation, such as replacing their home languages with English and, in some instances, Anglicizing their surnames. While such assimilation typically led to a devaluation of one's home culture, it carried the promise of increased economic opportunity and an elevated status. The distinction is important in that for some groups included in the U.S. Census Bureau definition of *White*, such as those of North African descent, the "benefits" of carrying a White identity are generally out of reach by virtue of their physical traits—most notably, skin color.

My use of the word *Whiteness*, in contrast to *White*, is to signify an ideological system in which a White racial and at times ethno-racial identification is utilized as the norm or standard and framed as superior to non-White identities. The word *system* is key to understanding the concept. While individuals can act in ways that perpetuate Whiteness, the emphasis is on influencing thought patterns and values as well as institutional policies and practices. A similar systems orientation can also apply to our understanding of racism. The sociologist Eduardo Bonilla-Silva (2012), among others, argues that rather than thinking of racism as the provenance of individual perpetrators, we should consider it as a *system*

---

[3]U.S. Census Bureau. (n.d.). *Race*. https://www.census.gov/quickfacts/fact/note/US/RHI625222

that relies on the cultural acceptance of superiority and inferiority bound to certain groups.

The ideology of Whiteness invokes a diminishment of non-White identities and cultures that plays out in multiple ways, such as devaluation, stereotyping, discrimination, and segregation. It manifests itself across our institutions, including education, banking, housing, and workplaces. It also permeates mainstream popular culture through the media. Whiteness elevates and idealizes aspects of Eurocentric culture including standards of beauty, language, and speech patterns (e.g., framing African American Vernacular English as "substandard" in comparison with Academic English). At the same time, darker skin hues are often exoticized or fetishized—yet another manifestation of degradation. And cultural artifacts of African, East Indian, and Asian origins are frequently appropriated: Think about trends in jewelry, hair styles and accoutrements, and clothing becoming "mainstream" over the years (e.g., Sari, corn rows, braids). The Whiteness ideology also accentuates and normalizes other identities as almost related offsprings reflective of the core White identity—identities such as heterosexuality, Christianity, and maleness.

Some readers may assume that the Whiteness ideology exists exclusively in White bodies. In fact, Whiteness lives within all of us in varying degrees whether we are aware of it or not, much like the air that we breathe. An example of this comes out of my consulting practice.

I met with a Black female middle school principal in the interest of addressing the lack of Black male students in her school who qualified for the advanced (or "gifted") math track. The school held a disproportionate pattern of White and Asian students over-represented in this math track. The principal asked me for feedback on an idea. Since she could not "find" any Black male students who wanted to participate in the gifted math class, she proposed launching a new program that honored giftedness in athletics. As you probably surmised, my reaction to this was less than positive.

Let's begin with the obvious. Such reasoning is grounded in the stereotypical belief that Black males have a "natural gift" in athletics. The flip side of this premise is that White students are more likely to be gifted in the cognitive domain. Whether she was aware of it or not, the principal fully embraced a Whiteness ideology by perpetuating a stereotypical, deficit-based belief of Black students as absent with cognitive ability. However, this story has even more layers. First, in a prior visit with this principal, while reviewing course grades of Black students, in fact, we *did* identify Black students who met the eligibility requirements for the gifted program. When I asked the principal about this finding, she responded, "I asked the students and their parents, but they did not want to be in those classes." The principal had missed the opportunity to inquire *why* they did not want to be in those classes. Among the many plausible explanations, for example, did the students feel uncomfortable joining classes in which the existing students already had formed social bonds by participating in gifted classes together since elementary school? And, if so, how might the school mitigate such discomfort? The principal had ample opportunity to learn from these students, but my concern centers on her interpretation of the students' position as a lack of initiative—that is, more deficit thinking. In fact, it seems that her criterion for access to more challenging coursework was based on a subjective standard of "initiative," rather than the students' capacity to meet such challenges evidenced by their prior performance in math classes. Ask yourself this: Since when is the much lauded practice of "engaging in productive struggle" the exclusive domain of White (and Asian) students?

A closer look at the alternative she proposed reveals additional flaws in the reasoning. What are the criteria for acceptance into a "gifted" athletics program? For that matter, what is the definition of "giftedness" in athletics? Nearly every athlete who excels at their sport will agree that their talents are largely a result of hard work, sustained practice, and (where available) good coaching. The idea that athletic (or cognitive) prowess is largely hereditary not only perpetuates troubling stereotypes but, in and of itself, will very likely erode the athlete's initiative to excel. After all, if we believe that our abilities are genetically hardwired, why bother making any effort to improve?

Finally, if we peel back yet another layer of this narrative, we get a better sense of what has transpired in this school and the surrounding community. The feeder pattern in this school district is all too common in many regions of the country. The White students attended an elementary school that is 90% White and affluent. Its parent–teacher association routinely raises over $75,000 annually through its activities, allocating the funds, in part, to pay for additional full-time gifted teachers. Consequently, a larger percentage of its students are enrolled in gifted classes. In contrast, the elementary schools that the Black students attended rely on restricted additional funds including the district's funding of a half-time-equivalent gifted teacher. Rather than question or challenge an obvious injustice, the principal accepted and justified it on the grounds that it is somehow "fair." In this case, she appears to have internalized a Whiteness ideology as evidenced by her belief that her Black students lack the initiative (or, perhaps, the capacity) to excel academically.

In sum, when we discuss the need to disrupt or unseat Whiteness in our schools and society at large, we are referring to a moral imperative to challenge an ideology or system used to discriminate against and otherwise oppress specific populations, most notably BIPOC Americans. Our example offers a vivid illustration of *disproportionality*, the subject matter of the next section of this chapter.

How Whiteness Shows Up in Our Schools and Beyond: Disproportionality

Disproportionality in K–12 education typically refers to the over- and underrepresentation of racial/ethnic minoritized groups in various contexts. Most notably, when we dig into school- and systemwide data, quite commonly we find an overrepresentation of BIPOC students in special education and an underrepresentation of the same students in gifted and talented, Advanced Placement (AP), and Honors programs and courses. BIPOC students also experience a disproportionately high rate of disciplinary referrals and suspensions when compared to their White and Asian counterparts. These patterns can be traced back to the early post–*Brown v. Board of Education* era, as evidenced by data collected in 1968 that estimated 60%–80% of students identified with cognitive disabilities were Black students from families considered low-income (Dunn, 1968). While subsequent studies point to some decline in such overrepresentation (Chinn & Hughes, 1987; Donovan & Cross, 2002), the patterns are still alarming when we consider that Black students currently comprise less than 15% of students enrolled in schools. In other words, the percentage of Black students enrolled in special education services continues to be disproportionate to their overall enrollment. Again, think back to the two pillars of *Brown*. Despite attempts to desegregate schools, ask yourself why such disproportionalities have persisted for so many years. If the structural changes in the interest of better school resources and facilities failed to eliminate these patterns, the question we must tackle as educators is whether we have done enough work to identify and eliminate the biases and deficit-based beliefs that impact such placements and referrals. The data suggest otherwise.

My work over the past two decades on addressing disproportionality in special education, discipline, and gifted/AP/Honors programs intersects both research and practice. I have worked with hundreds of schools and systems on investigating patterns of disproportionality and implementing reforms to eliminate them. Several key learnings have emerged from this work: (1) Gaps exist in the implementation of tiered intervention supports, special education referral and evaluation, discipline referral, and gifted identification, placement, and retention; and (2) the primary root cause of disproportionality is negative bias. More specifically, when educators filter their perceptions through a lens of Whiteness, students who don't fit the "norm" with respect to race and ethnicity—and (by extension), language, sexual orientation, or gender orientation—are judged as inferior to (and more harshly than) those who fit their preconception of what is "appropriate." Such instances frame cultural differences as deficits. My impetus for writing this book is to challenge us as educators to understand that the history of disproportionality cannot simply be solved by technical fixes and new and improved policies; rather, we must also tackle the biases that influence our mindsets and beliefs—biases that allow us to rationalize harmful and unjust educational processes, policies, procedures, and practices.

In my consulting work, I often sharpen my understanding of disproportionality and its roots by visiting classrooms. While disaggregated school-wide data on special education placement, disciplinary referrals, and the like offer a "big picture" view of disproportionality rates and patterns, the classroom visits allow me to see the more fine-grained, day-to-day textures of disproportionality. In the winter of 2021, I conducted classroom visits with a Black female principal. The student demographics in this school were 98% Black while the teaching staff was 80% White. The principal and I spoke a great deal about the quality of instruction. In particular, she repeatedly asked a very poignant question: "Do I have the right people in front of my kids?"

We walked into a fourth-grade classroom and observed a reading comprehension lesson for about 10 minutes. I signaled to the principal across the room that I was ready to go. Once outside the classroom, I asked her, "Is there a history in the classroom? Because something felt off in the interaction between the White female teacher and the Black and Brown students." The principal shared that, aside from some instructional gaps, the teacher had cultural conflicts with her students. The principal then shared that she had asked the teacher to build better social-emotional connections with her all–Black and Latinx class.

I then learned that during the month prior to my visit, in the interest of building such connections, the teacher had purchased a stuffed monkey for every student as a gift for the winter holiday season. While the students seemed to appreciate and enjoy interacting with the toy, the teacher's choice of gift is highly problematic. More specifically, it reveals the teacher's lack of understanding of the cultural history of her students—a painful, centuries-long history of comparing Blacks to primates based on erroneous perceptions of cognitive limitation and physical prowess. To put it mildly, her cultural frame, informed by the Whiteness ideology, lacked cross-cultural knowledge and experiences. In other words, she lived, absorbed, and universalized her experiences as a White woman. Educators who knowingly or unknowingly act on the assumption that their lived experiences are universal or "standard" place a crushing burden on their Black and Brown students. While this example may strike some readers as extreme, in my years of observing classrooms, I've witnessed countless examples of how Whiteness plays out in our schools.

The Shopping Cart Metaphor

For the last 20 years of my career, I have thought about, theorized on, and researched how Whiteness and its accompanying deficit-based framing of minoritized populations have become embedded in our approach to schooling. Where does this frame originate, and how do we continue to use it? I use the metaphor of a shopping cart to explain how we collect and perpetuate the beliefs that sustain frames of Whiteness, based on the idea that individuals travel throughout their days accumulating social and cultural experiences. Many of these experiences are monocultural, meaning they take place in segregated spaces. While this form of segregation is currently *de facto* (rather than *de jure* or governed by laws), it still has the effect of cultural isolation and *othering* those who are different from us. For a number of Americans, cross-cultural experiences (with the exception of casual encounters like passing differently complected people on the freeway or in the supermarket) occur relatively infrequently, which begs the question: If our shopping carts are filled with monocultural experiences, and if we draw from these experiences to make sense of our world, how can we truly understand and make sense of the experiences of those who differ from us?

For example, my youngest child, born female, disclosed at the age of 16 that they identified as a transgender male. My child had been on a long journey of self-reflection that culminated in their awareness of being trans. In retrospect, I realize that I was unprepared for this disclosure, in that the social and cultural experiences that lived in *my* shopping cart were grounded in the assumption of a gender binary. In other words, my lifelong experiences reinforced my belief that sex and gender are invariably tied together. More specifically, I had been living with the unchallenged belief that our reproductive organs, our physical appearance, our vocal tones, and other external traits signaled our gender identification and expression. All of this led me to the sobering realization that I had nothing in my shopping cart that helped me to understand and build cross-cultural connections with my child. The monocultural experiences that filled my shopping cart were products of a lifetime of interacting with cisgender communities. As a result of such limited (and limiting) experiences, I had "otherized" the trans community. My own journey impressed upon me the need to unpack my shopping cart and replace its contents with more culturally appropriate experiences that would help me interrogate and dismiss my deep-seated assumption of a gender binary.

My purpose in self-disclosing is to help you begin to engage in a similar journey of discovery. Think about it: How often in our society do we have the opportunity to unpack and replace the contents of our shopping carts? Or, more specifically, to unpack and replace beliefs, policies, and practices that manifest a Whiteness ideology that—as for the principal who wanted to provide her Black students with the "distinction" of an athletic giftedness label—allows us to rationalize a de facto policy of school segregation?

As much as we would like to believe that the passage of *Brown* in 1954 put the Jim Crow era behind us, the mechanism that rationalized the form of segregation that persists across our nation's schools—Whiteness—has yet to be removed and in fact lives well beyond our schools, extending across numerous events and artifacts of our daily existence. It took until 2020 (the year that George Floyd was murdered) for Johnson & Johnson to announce the addition of new skin tone colors to its Band-Aid product line. White actors and models still dominate commercials for beauty products. Employment practices stipulate "appropriate" hairstyles and clothing requirements as neat and presentable, yet who defines what constitutes neat or presentable? Our society has normalized a valuation of such Whiteness attributes as the "standard," and the shopping cart serves as a figurative tool for warehousing how we continuously draw and make meaning from this ideology. When a preponderance of Whiteness dominates our social shopping carts, it promotes and/or rationalizes our presumption of racial and ethnic hierarchies. Similar presumptions of superiority/inferiority live within us with respect to language, sexual orientation, and gender identities. In this manner, Whiteness as a cultural ideology highlights attributes related to and constructed from the social and cultural experiences of Whites and White identity as the standard.

When we reflect on the presence of Whiteness in our current K–12 landscape, we must come to terms with some challenging questions:

- What happens when we enter the schoolhouse with varying social experiences of race, ethnicity, language, sexuality, gender expression, and culture in our shopping carts?

- How do these mindsets and beliefs come into play when we interact with those whose lived experience is different and unfamiliar to us?

- How do these mindsets influence our academic expectations of students with differing racial, ethnic, linguistic, gender, and sexual identities?

- How has Whiteness ideology persisted and played out in our current school structures?

- How has the Whiteness ideology operated in recent state- and district-level policies that call for removal of books, lessons, and conversations that affirm the presence and value of marginalized identities?

In 1995, as a student teacher, I was assigned to a school with a predominantly White student body. During the interview process, the principal disclosed that I would be the first Black teacher who taught at this school in almost 20 years. At the end of my second week as a student teacher, one of the two White male teachers appointed as my "mentors" approached me with the following question: "Can you have a talk with the Black kids? You know, have a Black talk with them about how they should behave?" Just 21 years old at the time, I felt both baffled and offended that I was assigned such a role to play at this school. Beneath the surface of this request was the belief that I must somehow have the key to "reaching" Black students or, more pointedly, that I could "talk Black." I may have been baffled at the time, but in hindsight, I understand that this "mentor" teacher (like many others in this school) carried none of the tools, skills, language, cross-cultural competencies, or empathic capacity in his shopping cart needed to establish healthy relationships with his Black students. Unfortunately, such stereotypical beliefs about BIPOC students are not uncommon among educators with limited cross-cultural experiences. In this case, my "Black talks" were intended to show Black students how to be "good" students—in other words, to fit a specific norm of "good behavior" grounded in a Whiteness ideology. With time and effort, I believe that most educators can cultivate the awareness to identify how Whiteness informs our beliefs, policies, practices, and actions or, as in my example, to recognize how it informs the beliefs and actions of others in the school community. If you feel challenged by or uncomfortable with the questions posed earlier, remind yourself that cross-cultural experiences are within your reach!

How We Sustain Whiteness in Our Shopping Carts: Affinity and Associational Biases

An overarching premise of this book is that by accumulating more cross-cultural experiences in our shopping carts, we can challenge the deep-seated beliefs and stereotypes that harm our minoritized students through our policies, practices, words, and deeds. Social psychology research highlights the significance of such experiences in dispelling stereotypes (Pettigrew & Tropp, 2006; Rasmussen & Sieck, 2015). In fact, as an American society, we have limited cross-cultural exposure, as evidenced by one of the most substantive support networks in our lives: our closest friends. A 2022 study from the Public Religion Research Institute found that Whites report having social friendships that are 90% White; 67% reported having *only* White friends. Older Whites had more segregated friendship circles than their younger counterparts. In contrast, the same study found that non-White populations generally maintain much more cross-cultural friendships.

In fact, these friendship patterns demonstrate two important ways that Whiteness sustains its effect: *affinity bias* and *associational bias*. Affinity describes our tendency to gravitate toward people like us. We all have affinity groups, and one of mine is runners. I think of myself as a serious runner. I began running when I was 12 years old in the mid-1980s when children were required to run one mile as part of the presidential fitness test. I met the benchmark of running faster than 7 minutes and 11 seconds but, more importantly, fell in love with running. Since then, I competed in track for nearly 10 years in high school and college, and after college I ran (and continue to run) hundreds of 5- and 10-mile races and half-marathons. Not surprisingly, I always gravitate toward other runners. We speak a special language to each other and share the experience of on- and off-season training. This affinity leans into favoring each other. But affinity bias means more than sharing common interests and passions. Affinity bias serves to support our need to belong and feel connected to people who will empathize with our experiences and worldviews. Affinity refers to the ways in which we favor in-group members. Our positive bias in favor of such members manifests in our willingness to give them extra leeway or permission. For example, if street closures catch me in traffic on the day of a marathon, I am far more patient and forgiving than those who don't share my affinity bias. In other words, we think more favorably of "folks like us." Among neuroscientific evidence for this phenomenon,

MRI data confirm that when we think about or interact with in-group members, our brains light up in similar patterns to those that form when we talk or think about ourselves (Molenberghs & Louis, 2018).

This affinity bias also affects how we explain crises or challenging events, viewing the in-group in a more favorable light compared to out-group members. For example, the national opioid crisis of our current century has been framed as a tragedy caused by pharmaceutical companies' manipulation of individuals. Compare this explanation of what amounts to a national addiction with the far less sympathetic narrative of the "crack" drug war of the 1980s. The news stories of the 1980s framed crack users as degenerates and criminals. Attribution, or who was framed as "at fault," was based on in-group bias in the case of the opioid crisis and out-group bias in the case of the crack drug war. Crack, a relatively cheap drug, was most commonly associated with Black Americans, whereas opioid addiction was more commonly associated with White Americans. (A similar dynamic was at work in the 1980s and 1990s when criminal sentencing for crack users was far more harsh than sentencing for powder cocaine users.)

Our shopping carts are filled with examples of beliefs that reflect our affinity biases. You may consciously or subconsciously believe someone is smart or capable of doing a specific job simply because they attended the same university as you or because they share your age, ethnic, sexual, or gender identification. You can enter a room and only see the people like you, failing even to notice the presence of other people. This form of bias allows for the maintenance of similar affinities. A common example of affinity bias in the world of K–12 is hiring teachers who are "like you," share your belief system, or have similar training.

The effect of this affinity bias also appears in how we treat students in our schools. For instance, I arrived early for a data meeting with an elementary school principal and noticed the White female principal meeting with two White female students. Once the students left and I entered the principal's office, I asked if everything was okay, and she shared that she had just met with two students who had a "scuffle" and were "mean-spirited." Later we discussed the discipline data from the prior three months of school that showed that each month the office discipline referrals were primarily male (i.e., above 80%) and involved "disrespect," "disorderly conduct," and so on. I asked her if "mean-spirited" described a type of infraction. Did being mean-spirited and engaging in a scuffle warrant an office referral, or would she give the two White female students a pass, based on an affinity bias? Think about your own school context: Are male students more susceptible to an affinity bias that frames them as a greater "physical threat" than their female peers and, consequently, places them at greater risk of office referrals and/or suspensions?

Like other manifestations of Whiteness, in-group favoritism rationalizes superiority over those outside the affinity group. For instance, hiring practices may lead to the exclusion of teachers who "don't fit our culture," are "stand-offish," or did not attend schools familiar to us. In another example, a White, Italian-identifying male assistant superintendent of a district once approached me in an attempt to diversify the district's teaching workforce. This administrator wanted to know if I knew anything about historically Black colleges and universities (HBCUs) and Hispanic-serving institutions (HSIs). He disclosed to me, "I've never heard of these schools. How long have they been around, and are they any good?"

This leader's question regarding the quality of these institutions reflects both affinity and associational biases. His affinity was toward familiar schools, and its effect was the assumption that applicants who attended these unfamiliar schools were inadequately prepared for teaching positions in his school. Associational bias, also referred to as confirmatory bias, occurs when an individual seeks information that confirms or maintains a set of beliefs, values, or perceptions associated with specific groups. These tend to be stereotypical ideas of an out-group (Oswald & Grosjean, 2004). Associational bias is derived from experiences and information that we rack up during our life span and uses stereotypes as a shorthand way to simplify the information. For instance, we may demonstrate our associational bias when we see a person at a grocery store paying with a cash assistance card or EBT[4] card, and we begin to examine their food choices; when we are in grade-level meetings discussing students needing support, and someone shares that a child lives in a trailer park; or when an assistant superintendent questions the value of Black and Latinx higher education institutions.

We carry a litany of concepts and assumptions about identities and, without realizing it, seek confirmation of these assumptions. In a 2016 study conducted by the Yale Child Study Center,[5] Gilliam and colleagues asked preschool teachers to watch a video of students and identify "misbehaviors." In fact, no students actually misbehaved in the video.

---

[4]U.S. Department of Agriculture Food and Nutrition Service. (2023, October 3). *What Is Electronic Benefits Transfer (EBT)?* https://www.fns.usda.gov/snap/ebt
[5]Gilliam, W. S., Maupin, A. N., Reyes, C. R., Accavitti, M., & Shic, F. (2016, September 28). *Do early educators' implicit biases regarding sex and race relate to behavior expectations and recommendations of preschool expulsions and suspensions?* Yale Child Study Center. https://files-profile.medicine.yale.edu/documents/75afe6d2-e556-4794-bf8c-3cf105113b7c?sv

However, the teachers were three times more likely to identify boys and boys of color with behavior problems.

These associational biases are fed to us via a healthy diet of stereotypes, many of which show up in media and other artifacts of popular culture. Consider the case of American Girl dolls. My youngest child took an interest in these between six and eight years old, and in the interest of accommodating her interest, I decided to investigate. I discovered that these dolls are quite expensive and, at the time, occupied an entire multistory New York City building. The first time I visited the American Girl store, I was struck by what appeared to be an affluent and predominantly White clientele milling around the floors. The doll demographic matched that of the clientele in that eight of them appeared to be White and the remaining three (one each Black, Native American, and Mexican American) clearly were not. They differed in their respective stories, printed on accompanying placards. The White American girl stories, while set in different eras (e.g., World War II, the 1950s), were remarkably similar to one another in that the characters seemed to enjoy relatively comfortable lives. These stories stood in stark contrast to the story of the sole Black doll depicted as an escaped slave who, along with her mother, gets separated from her father and brother—a story of loss and struggle. I should acknowledge that since my visit to the store, the company has introduced additional Black dolls including Claudie, whose story is written by Brit Bennett, a Black author, and centers on being a Black girl full of joy in the 1920s.

With that said, the narratives behind these products feed an associational bias that characterizes the stories of BIPOC people by sadness and struggle. The habit of associational bias extends well beyond toy manufacturers and appears across our social institutions including law enforcement, employment settings, and schools. For example, police officers looking for "suspicious behaviors" may orient themselves toward individuals who fit their association of suspicious behaviors and ignore or excuse the same suspicious behaviors of individuals who fit their in-group schema. In schools, when intervention study teams focus on a student exhibiting skill gaps, they consider "home environment" factors or "student disposition" for students outside of their affinity circles; in contrast, such considerations are infrequent for in-group students. Associational bias is also quite common in the world of K–12 practice. I recall attending a meeting with a school's equity team about the root causes of their disproportionality patterns. The psychologist on the team argued that the continuous exposure to lead paint and polluted water caused the school's overidentification of Black students with intellectual disabilities and emotional dysregulation despite not having any knowledge of where the students lived.

Patterns emerge in schools that further reinforce associational bias. For instance, if we continuously see White and Asian (specifically, Chinese and Japanese) children in gifted classrooms, we develop an associational frame. We develop a belief of what giftedness looks like based on overrepresentation of White and Asian students in gifted programs. When I ask teachers of gifted, advanced, AP, Honors, and International Baaccalaureate programs what qualities make a student succeed in these classes, they often refer to social or cultural qualities: "shows initiative," "has a desire for the extra work," "is curious to do more," or "demonstrates strong work ethic." Even if these attributes were "objective," the disproportionate pattern of White and Asian students means these attributes are earmarked as an associational bias about these groups. Simultaneously, when we are continuously exposed to deficit narratives about other (non-White) groups that portray them as lazy, irresponsible, economically stunted, and so on, we form an associational bias that feeds deficit-based assumptions about their behavior and cognitive abilities. (For example, tune into such media outlets as Fox News and Newsmax that depict non-White, non-straight, nonbinary, non-Christian, non-middle-class populations in a less-than-flattering light, albeit often through coded language like *inner city* to signify Black, low-income neighborhoods.)

During a data analysis meeting, I shared the patterns of behavioral referrals by sex, and a White male principal raised his hand and argued, "That happens because boys have horseplay in their DNA." In that moment, this male principal maintained an associational bias about boys that included viewing their behavior as nature-driven. In other words, they are just "hardwired" to misbehave. Victim-blaming language like "They just can't help themselves" not only absolves K–12 professionals of any responsibility but also suggests other deficit-driven distortions like "Those kids misbehave like that because they come from low-income neighborhoods" or "Low-income kids are inherently traumatized and thus carry cognitive and/or behavioral limitations." A monoglossic ideology (O. García & Torres-Guevara, 2009)—another extension of Whiteness—is evidenced in such statements as "Why can't they just speak English in the hallways?" or (by association) "Did they come here illegally to take our services?" The power of such associational bias is it is (1) deeply embedded in an individual's shopping cart and unless disrupted will continuously be utilized to perpetuate inequities; and (2) used to attribute disparities to cultural or environmental factors, rather than barriers to access and opportunity. The dangers of such toxic narratives extend well beyond individual harm and into the institutions and systems that govern us in that we used them to rationalize structural inequities such as discriminatory economic, social, and educational policies. Rather than call these policies into question, we place the blame on those who bear the brunt of such discrimination and are framed as lacking intelligence, initiative, or "grit" or simply as victims of "tough luck."

All these forms of bias are ever-present in our shopping carts and activated at various times when we enter schools. The problem with such biases is that they falsely attribute "blame" to our students, to our students' families, and to the communities in which they reside and ultimately rationalize inequitable systems, policies, and practices never designed to serve these students in the first place. Moreover, such systemic failures have harmed generations of minoritized students and families.

K–12 professionals can and should play a role in addressing them, beginning with challenging our own biases. Admittedly, this is hard work—especially given our current sociopolitical climate—but I want to believe that most of us in this field share a genuine desire to realize the promise of *Brown* by once and for all eliminating what Judge Huxton called the "sense of inferiority" that continues to live in so many of our children today.

Chapter Road Map

Several chapters of this book are devoted to identifying three common, but rarely explored, belief systems that perpetuate Whiteness in our schools and beyond: *colorblindness*, *deficit thinking*, and *poverty disciplining*. As I discussed in my previous Corwin book, *Solving Disproportionality and Achieving Equity* (Fergus, 2016a), these beliefs manifest themselves in educational practice in ways that create barriers to success for all students—particularly those who are historically marginalized. For instance, think about how deficit thinking informs our attitudes about behavioral expectations for our students. Such expectations, for the most part culture-bound, include presumptions about what is "loud," "threatening," or "standing too close," and even the proper way to sit in a chair. At a time when our attempts to "fix" underserved schools and student populations involve silver-bullet behavior management programs, the need to expose and unseat these beliefs is more urgent than ever. Rather than searching for the silver bullet of the month, I challenge you to unpack the baggage of segregated lives and to interrogate your own lived experiences as the source of the bias-based beliefs crammed into your shopping cart. In doing so, you will begin to see the world differently, through a cross-cultural lens that frees you to envision a "new normal" in which our children are affirmed and valued and can truly grow into their best selves.

Over the course of my research, I've collected survey data from over 4,000 educators that highlight their beliefs. These beliefs accumulate in the personal shopping cart of the Teach for America White male teacher from rural all-White Kansas assigned to teach in an all-Black New Orleans school; the Long Island, New York, suburban White female now teaching in the all–Black and Latinx South Bronx; and countless educators with similarly limited cross-cultural exposure. My work with these educators has affirmed my belief that cross-cultural skills and knowledge are within every educator's reach. The remainder of this book will serve as your guide to unpacking your shopping cart and developing these skills and dispositions.

Chapter 1 provides a historical overview of schooling in the United States and the progenitors to a system that continues to perpetuate Whiteness. In particular, it outlines laws and policies that supported and sustained superiority of White identification through the limitation of educational facilities, resources, curriculum, instruction, and personnel for Mexican, Black, and Indigenous/Native American populations. We need to understand these early strategies for cementing the Whiteness ideology in order to understand the way it has metastasized.

Chapter 2 provides a deeper exploration of the valuation of Whiteness including the manner in which it is fueled by fears of losing resources and monopoly, social threat of "the other," and fear of no longer being the standard of normalcy by which others are judged. We will understand how Whiteness has hampered the ability of educators to develop the cross-cultural understanding that will enable them to form healthy relationships and enhance their pedagogical effectiveness with students who don't look like them.

Chapters 3 and 4 focus on the aforementioned bias-based mindsets: colorblindness, deficit thinking, and poverty disciplining. Each mindset provides a rationalization for the persistence of the Whiteness ideology in our schools and beyond. These chapters are organized to provide an understanding of the mindsets, their genesis, and the ways in which they persist. The chapters also include vignettes intended to support your cross-cultural skill development, specifically by examining how these beliefs show up in our schools and most importantly how you can begin to replace them.

Finally, Chapter 5 provides a framework for a deliberate development of cross-cultural skills and dispositions that interrupt the valuation of Whiteness and devaluation of all other groups and recenter the notion of humanity in our educational equity beliefs that *Brown v. Board of Education* charged us to implement.

Reflection Questions

These reflection questions are intended to encourage unpacking and replacing the experiences in our shopping carts.

1. What is your experience of disproportionality in your school?

2. What is your prior experience with talking or hearing about Whiteness ideology?

3. What are your key affinity groups? What positive orientations do you have about these affinity groups?

4. What are some of your associational biases? How do you address them?

5. What were your friendship groups in elementary school, middle school, high school, and college? What were your friendship groups and neighbors in the community you grew up in?

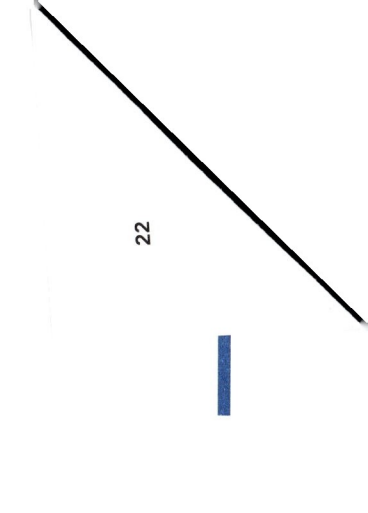

History of Using Whiteness to Create Ethno-Racial Segregation

From School Segregation to Integration: How Whiteness Limited Our Impact

> "Now slavery as an institution has been overthrown, but slavery as an idea still lives in the American republic." (F. E. W. Harper, January 1867, Philadelphia National Hall)

Frances Ellen Watkins Harper, a Black poet and author, spoke these words at the Social, Civil, and Statistical Association of the Colored People in Philadelphia.[1] Harper hints that slavery continued to have roots because the Whiteness ideology that justified slavery continued to exist in the country—abolishing slavery did not remove Whiteness as the cultural center. The Emancipation Proclamation abolished slavery but did not provide a proclamation abandoning Whiteness. As educators, we need to maintain this important realization; the educational system, just like many other systems in U.S. society, was universalized based on the experiences—and need to reinforce the social and economic interests—of White-identifying individuals.

In this chapter, I outline the history of using Whiteness to create the educational system favoring Whites through the segregation of Native Americans, Mexican Americans, and African Americans. Specifically, I discuss how Whiteness ideology expanded from framing light skin color as the signifier

---

[1] Gardner, E. (2017, Summer). Frances Ellen Watkins Harper's "National Salvation": A rediscovered lecture on Reconstruction. *Common Place: The Journal of Early American Life*, *17*(4). http://commonplace.online/article/vol-17-no-4-gardner/

of superiority to including other cultural features (English language, mannerisms, family connections, individualism, American patriotism, meritocracy, etc.), language, and citizenship status.[2] I intend to provide the context for how Whiteness was utilized to create our educational system, in order to understand how its contemporary operation directly resulted from this initial architecture; our society attempted, adjusted, adapted, learned, and morphed its ideas of education to serve the ideology of Whiteness.

An important concept to understand involves the use of laws and policies to cement the validity of Whiteness. In other words, laws (legal frameworks for rights) and policies (regulatory actions that support implementation of laws) regarding services such as schooling, voting, housing, and employment were written based on "universal" experiences of White-identifying individuals to reinforce that universality of White identity. An outgrowth of these laws and policies included the strengthening of affinity and associational biases toward non-Whites, non-Christians, non-heterosexuals, and others. During Reconstruction (1865–1877) and post-Reconstruction, Whiteness tools—affinity and associational bias—operated in full action. For instance, since African Americans received full citizenship on July 9, 1868, via the Fourteenth Amendment, Whites utilized other means to sustain segregation, such as curtailing the rights of Black Americans in order to manage their movements. In fact, legislators inserted a provision in the Thirteenth Amendment that servitude or slavery can be invoked for individuals who commit crimes:

> Neither slavery nor involuntary servitude, except as a punishment for crime whereof the party shall have been duly convicted, shall exist within the United States, or any place subject to their jurisdiction.[3]

This provision led to the development of convict leasing. In essence, individuals convicted of crimes would be leased to farms, companies, or other firms to serve as labor. These companies would pay a fee to local governments for using this labor owned by the state—an emerging strategy for incarcerating Black people. The crimes of which courts found Black people guilty included walking on someone's grass, looking incorrectly at a White person, or assembling day or night while not having gainful employment papers, which meant being employed by a White person (Conwill &

---

[2]Though not the central focus of this book, sexuality, gender, and gender identification were also expanded into the camp of Whiteness ideology.
[3]U.S. National Archives and Records Administration. (2022, May 10). *13th Amendment to the U.S. Constitution: Abolition of slavery (1865)*. https://www.archives.gov/milestone-documents/13th-amendment

Gardullo, 2021). Such policy actions and many others like these perpetuated an associational bias toward Black Americans as deviant.

Additional elements of the social slavery that Harper references involve the development of "Black codes." Used by municipalities as policy tools to minimize the assembly and protest of Black people, these codes included being deemed vagrant for not paying child support, as well as not being allowed to quit a job before the expiration of their contract, rent or own property, or own any type of weapon including a knife (Conwill & Gardullo, 2021). These habits of segregation were justified by beliefs of inferiority toward Black, Indigenous, and Mexican populations and continued throughout the rest of the 19th and 20th centuries. In outlining this history I intend to reveal how Whiteness ideology has been sewn into the fabric of the American psyche, and make clear that the educational system was organized to serve its students based on this ideology. The remainder of this chapter provides an overview of Whiteness ideology as utilized in the educational trajectory of Indigenous, Mexican, and Black populations.

Indigenous Schooling: Removing the "Savagery" to Dispossess Them of Their Lands

The enslavement of Indigenous populations in the United States operated differently yet from a similar tenet—maintain separation, educate them in order to make them civilized, and diminish their Indigenous culture. As early as the 1700s, the U.S. government developed plans for "civilizing" Native Americans. The rationale for this assimilationist approach was twofold: (1) enable White colonizers to possess the lands owned by Native Americans through "dispossession," and (2) tame the "savage" culture, viewed as threatening to White colonizers, of Native Americans. In an 1803 confidential message, President Thomas Jefferson provided such a rationalization for segregating and civilizing Native Americans:

> To encourage them to abandon hunting, to apply to the raising stock, to agriculture, and domestic manufacture, and thereby prove to themselves that less land and labor will maintain them in this better than in their former mode of living. The extensive forests necessary in the hunting life will then become useless, and they will see advantage in exchanging them for the means of improving their farms and of increasing their domestic comforts.[4]

---

[4]Newland, B. (2022, May). *Federal Indian Boarding School Initiative: Investigative report*. U.S. Department of the Interior, Bureau of Indian Affairs. https://www.bia.gov/sites/default/files/dup/inline-files/bsi_investigative_report_may_2022_508.pdf, p. 21.

Through his presidential pulpit, Jefferson further anointed the strategy of segregating Native Americans in off-reservation boarding schools. In his 1801 congressional address, President Jefferson articulated the need to civilize Indigenous people:

> Among our Indian neighbors also, a spirit of peace and friendship generally prevails and I am happy to inform you that the continued efforts to introduce among them the implements and the practice of husbandry, and of the household arts, have not been without success; that they are becoming more and more sensible of the superiority of this dependence for clothing and subsistence over the precarious resources of hunting and fishing.[5]

Over the next nearly 100 years, the U.S. government continued this strategy of Native American land dispossession through assimilation, debt accumulation, and boarding schools for their children. In 1886, a U.S. Indian agent described in his notes the lengths to which they went to kidnap Native American children for these boarding schools:

> I found the attendance at the boarding school about half of what it should be, and at once set about increasing it to the full capacity of the accommodation. This I found extremely difficult. When called upon for children, the chiefs, almost without exception, declared there were none suitable for school in their camps. Everything in the way of persuasion and argument having failed, it became necessary to visit the camps unexpectedly with a detachment of Indian police, and seize such children as were proper and take them away to school, willing or unwilling. Some hurried their children off to the mountains or hid them away in camp, and the Indian police had to chase and capture them like so many wild rabbits.[6]

The prevalence of these boarding schools is astounding and served as part of the process to dispossess Native Americans of their land and to assimilate their children because of the associational bias of "savagery" with Native Americans. In other words, assimilating Indigenous children to "American" cultural habits provides a platform for the children to assimilate their identity to serve "American" priorities, which include the occupation of lands owned by others. In a 2021 report,

---

[5]Ibid., p. 26.
[6]Ibid., p. 29.

commissioned by the Secretary of the Department of the Interior, the U.S. government acknowledged that between 1819 and 1969, "the Federal Indian boarding school system consisted of 408 Federal schools across 37 states or then-territories, including 21 schools in Alaska and 7 schools in Hawaii."[7] The states with the most schools included Oklahoma (76), Arizona (47), New Mexico (43), South Dakota (30), Minnesota (21), Alaska (21), Montana (16), Washington (15), California (12), and North Dakota (12). These schools involved removing any remnants of Indigenous culture—language, hair, clothing, and family connections. Images shared in the 2021 commissioned report and related images catalogued by the Library of Congress show Apache children before and after arriving at one of the boarding schools (see Figure 1.1).

FIGURE 1.1 Apache Children Before and After Entering Off-Reservation Boarding School

Source: Ciricahua Apaches at the Carlisle Indian School, as they looked upon arrival at the School, 1885 or 1886 [Photograph]. Library of Congress. https://www.loc.gov/item/2006679977/; and *Ciricahua Apaches at the Carlisle Indian School, after 4 months of training at the School* [Photograph]. Library of Congress. https://www.loc.gov/item/2006679978/

We learn from this process of school segregation with Indigenous children that Whiteness ideology was used to define the cultural features of Native Americans as inferior. We simultaneously learn that White identification involved cultural features such as uniformity in dress, English language dominance, and superiority to Native Americans. Finally, we begin to understand the building of Native boarding school curriculum to center White identity-based experiences as the trough in which science, social studies, reading and English language arts, mathematics, and arts content is developed.

---

[7] Ibid., p. 82.

> **Shopping Cart Exploration Pause**
>
> 1. Take a moment and imagine how Indigenous parents experienced their children being sent away to these schools. Now also imagine the individuals who enacted such processes. How do you imagine they rationalized their actions? Did they view themselves as doing the "right thing" because they maintained an associational bias about Indigenous populations?
>
> 2. What parts of Indigenous history are familiar to you? When did you learn them?
>
> 3. How do we introduce this history in elementary, middle, and high school?
>
> 4. Review your novels, read-aloud books, bulletin boards, and other resources. Where do you see the representations of Indigenous populations?

Mexicans in Schools: Education for English Only

After the Treaty of Guadalupe Hidalgo in 1848, the United States took lands from Mexico that now comprise Texas, New Mexico, Arizona, Utah, Colorado, and California. According to Article VIII of this treaty, Mexicans living in the lands ceded by the Mexican government would be granted U.S. citizenship and retain the ownership of their properties.[8] This element of the treaty proved to be an interesting quandary because during that time only Whites could own land and be citizens; thus, Mexicans were officially denoted as White but socially ascribed as Mexican (Donato & Hanson, 2012). Between 1848 and 1930, the U.S. Census Bureau identified Mexicans as White, and Mexican was included as an option in the 1930 Census but then removed until 1970. Figure 1.2 shows the 1850 Census form; column 6 shows only three "colors" or races—White, Black, and Mulatto (mixed White and Black).

---

[8]U.S. National Archives and Records Administration. (2022, September 20). *Treaty of Guadalupe Hidalgo (1848)*. https://www.archives.gov/milestone-documents/treaty-of-guadalupe-hidalgo

FIGURE 1.2 1850 Census Form

1850 Federal Census

STATE					MICROFILM SERIES	
COUNTY OR PARISH		TOWNSHIP/TOWN/ OR CITY		DATE OF ENUMERATION		PAGE

Line Number	Dwelling houses numbered in the order of visitation.	Family numbered in the order of visitation.	The name of every person whose usual place of abode on the 1st day of June, 1850, was in this family.	DESCRIPTION			Profession, occupation, or trade of each person over 15 years of age.	Value of real estate owned.	Place of Birth. Naming the State, Territory, or Country.	Married within the year.	At school within the last year.	Persons over 20 years of age who cannot read and write.	Deaf and dumb, blind, insane, idiotic, pauper, or convict.
				Age.	Sex.	Color. { White, Black, or Mulatto							
	1	2	3	4	5	6	7	8	9	10	11	12	13
1.													
2.													
3.													
4.													
5.													
6.													
7.													
8.													
9.													
10.													
11.													
12.													

National Archives and Records Administration www.archives.gov NA 14083 (04-09)

Source: U.S. National Archives and Records Administration. (2022, August 23). 1850 Census records. https://www.archives.gov/research/census/1850

Figure 1.3 demonstrates the section requesting information regarding Mexican identification. After 1970, the Census placed Mexicans and other Latinx-identified groups in an Ethnicity category.

FIGURE 1.3   1970 Census Questionnaire

Name of person on line (1) of page 2

Last name   First name   Initial

13a. Where was this person born? *If born in hospital, give State or country where mother lived. If born outside U.S., see instruction sheet; distinguish Northern Ireland from Ireland (Eire).*

○ This State

OR

(Name of State or foreign country; or Puerto Rico, Guam, etc.)

b. Is this person's origin or descent— *(Fill one circle)*

○ Mexican   ○ Central or South American
○ Puerto Rican   ○ Other Spanish
○ Cuban   ○ No, none of these

Source: U.S. Census Bureau. (2022, December 5). *1970 Census questionnaire.* https://www.census.gov/history/www/through_the_decades/questionnaires/1970_1.html

It is important to note that Whiteness ideology at times served as the basis for creating laws that were also difficult for policies focusing on segregation to support. In the case of Mexicans following the Treaty of Guadalupe Hidalgo (1848), the United States made Mexicans citizens, but citizenry was only socially allowed for White-identifying individuals. Thus, Whiteness ideology instead helped to justify the development of another identity marker for segregation—language. Various states developed laws and policies to make that distinction. In other words, the English language became a calling card of nationalism, at that time framed by White-identified individuals; suffice it to say using language to segregate became another strategy to promote Whiteness ideology.

In 1855, the California state legislature amended their new state constitution to include a provision in which all proceedings and services in the state would be in English only. This meant the educational process for those who identified as Mexican American was premised on language segregation. David García (2018) documents various case studies throughout California in which Mexican Americans were segregated using language via housing and schooling. One particular case study occurs in Oxnard, California. In the early 1900s, the school superintendent, mayor, and other city officials organized the city services, including the school system, to align their segregation of Mexicans. One of those White architects, as D. García highlights, is Richard Haydock, who served as principal and superintendent of Oxnard schools. He spoke most explicitly about a need for the Oxnard community to segregate Mexicans in order to maintain the community as "clean":

> The ignorant are allowed to live and breed under conditions that become a threat and a menace to the welfare of the community. . . . Many cases of filth and disease and contagion are found by us in the school work. We suggest to these Mexican people that they care for themselves but they do nothing. The personal health of the Mexican children in the grammar school affects every child in the school. (D. García, 2018, p. 12)

D. García (2018) notes that the organization of both laws and policy involved the following: In mid-February 1917, the plans for paving Oxnard only included the White neighborhoods; during an outbreak of the flu, the local hospital did not permit Mexicans to be admitted, and instead city police opened a makeshift hospital at a detention center; and the city planned for creating segregated children's playgrounds. Countless such case studies illustrate the ways in which laws and policies were utilized to operationalize the critical elements of Whiteness ideology—sustaining a singular White-affinity community in its purest forms and highlighting the inferiority of BIPOC communities.

In 1910, after achieving statehood, New Mexico also minted new English-only policies to limit the incorporation of Mexican populations; "that provision shall be made for the establishment and for public maintenance of a system of public schools, which shall be open to all the children of said State and free from sectarian control, and that said schools shall always be conducted in English."[9] Overall, the framing of language as reasoning for segregation was used to illustrate a level of "nativism" expected of an American identity. In order words, being American meant speaking English, considered the hallmark language of White identification. The storied segregation of Mexicans illustrates for us how Whiteness ideology became imbued with English language as a cultural feature to maintain for the purity of the race.

---

[9] New Mexico Constitution, *Article XXI: Compact with the United States § 4 Public schools*. https://law.justia.com/constitution/new-mexico/article-xxi/section-4/

> ### Shopping Cart Exploration Pause
>
> 1. Take a moment and imagine how speaking another language was conveyed to parents as a problem. Now also imagine the individuals who enacted such processes. How do you imagine they rationalized their actions? Did they view themselves as doing the "right thing" because they maintained an associational bias about Mexican American populations?
>
> 2. What parts of Mexican American history are familiar to you? When did you learn them?
>
> 3. How do we introduce this history in elementary, middle, and high school?
>
> 4. Review your novels, read-aloud books, bulletin boards, and other resources. Where do you see the representations of Mexican American populations?

Virginia: State-Sponsored Skin-Color-Based Exclusion of Black Students

The case of segregation among African Americans centered on using race or skin color as a proxy to determine educational services. That such segregation occurred prior to *Brown v. Board of Education* but continued after the ruling is an important point to understand about Whiteness ideology; although educational laws and policies were organized for the purpose of skin color segregation prior to 1954, afterward we learned the ideology was able to adapt itself post *Brown*. The prevailing memory or story we carry as citizens is that once the ruling was passed a level of resistance emerged to end segregated schools; however, we don't necessarily recognize that it centered on sustaining the valuation of White children's school experiences. This resistance was very much bound to White families drawing from a shopping cart filled with associational and affinity bias experiences that reinforced this valuation. Any move to shift or upend their shopping carts, such as school desegregation and integration, was an assault on their way of life; a way of life promoted in parenting guides (DuRocher, 2011). A well-circulated adage nicely encapsulates why White families pushed back on desegregation as an educational equity: "When you're accustomed to privilege, equity feels like oppression." School desegregation and integration were perceived as oppressing their privileged experience—an experience of Whiteness is the ability to continuously define itself as the norm for everyone (M. Bell, 2021) and as a tool to monopolize resources (E. K. Wilson, 2021). The image[10] in Figure 1.4 reflects White protesters, reporters, and plainclothes police in Nashville, Tennessee, in September 1957, reflective of similar tactics in Virginia.

FIGURE 1.4 White Protesters, Reporters, and Plainclothes Police Outside Glenn Elementary in Nashville, Tennessee, September 1957

Source: © Nashville Public Library, Special Collections.

This community rallied the majority of the White community to protest the integration of schools including appearing on days when Black parents were registering their first graders (see Figure 1.5).

---

[10]Egerton, J. (2009, May 4). Walking into history: The beginning of school desegregation in Nashville. *Southern Spaces*. https://southernspaces.org/2009/walking-history-beginning-school-desegregation-nashville/

FIGURE 1.5 Fred Stroud Leads Protest Against Desegregation, Nashville, Tennessee, 1957

Source: © Nashville Public Library, Special Collections.

Demonstrating these images provides us an imagery of how communities throughout the country rallied around sustaining White schools; despite knowing about the unequal facilities, they were not rallying to improve schools for Black, Mexican, or Indigenous students. Kristina DuRocher (2011) documents in *Raising Racists: The Socialization of White Children in the Jim Crow South* that White communities organized churches, neighborhood associations, and their parenting to reinforce the importance and valuation of White children:

> White southern parents' instruction in regulating relations between the races was grounded in a highly idealized and nostalgic vision of a paternalistic white society. The ideological objective of this instruction, however unrealistic, was that the New South should replicate the romanticized social order of slavery. The lessons that shaped young children's identity were primarily racial, not surprising in a racially segregated society with idealized expectations of white masculinity and femininity tied to morality and contrasted with African American degradation. (p. 14)

Thus, imagining society post *Brown* needs to emphasize an understanding that dismantling segregated schools was also about dismantling segregated parenting, neighborhood associations, golf courses, playgrounds, and other institutions. As an example, Virginia residents, like many from both southern and northern states, found ways to resist the *Brown* decision. On October 26, 1954, the Defenders of State Sovereignty and Individual Liberties was formed to oppose the *Brown* decision. The non-profit organization maintained specific values as part of their charter (see Figure 1.6). They believed in "the preservation of racial integrity, an education for all children, and a society based on racial separateness."

FIGURE 1.6   Charter of Defenders of State Sovereignty

"Defenders of State Sovereignty and Individual Liberties"

Chartered in Virginia on October 26, 1954

WE ARE

Non-Profit
Non-Political

WE BELIEVE

In the Sovereignty of the Several States;

In certain liberties for the individual citizens of these states;

In the preservation of racial integrity;

In an education for **all** children;

In a society based on racial separateness;

In the seperation of church and state;

In the precious heritage handed down to us by our forefathers;

Very sincerely, that our objectives are in the best interest of both races.

WE INTEND

To use every lawful, honorable and peaceful means to maintain the above principles;

To inform the people as to their inherent rights;

To give the best possible leadership to the thousands of people in Virginia who feel as we do, and who will unite with us.

We have thousands of members from all parts of the state. Included in this membership are U. S. Congressmen, many members of our State Legislature, County and City officials, Judges, lawyers, doctors, ministers, educators, other leading business and professional men and women, housewives and people from all walks of life.

If you believe in these principles and would like to join us, or if you desire more information, fill out the enclosed card and mail to your local Chapter or to William E. Maxey, Jr., P. O. Box 1916, Richmond 19, Virginia. We will be pleased to furnish you with applications and material.

Source: Defenders of State Sovereignty and Individual Liberties, Courtesy of Special Collections and University Archives, Old Dominion University Libraries

This citizen-based organization, similar to the type that emerged in the 2010s and 2020s (e.g., Oath Keepers, Proud Boys, Tea Party, Moms for Liberty), purported to preserve their worldview, which included a valuation of Whiteness cloaked in language such as "individual liberties," "American values," and "freedom principles." Such organizations received further support from governmental actors as well, similar to the current actions seen in the banning of discussions regarding race, diversity, gender expression, and sexuality (e.g., Tennessee, Florida, Texas, Oklahoma). For instance, in 1958, the Norfolk Public Schools sought an injunction to prevent the integration of 17 Black children into their White middle and high schools. The district hoped to halt efforts to integrate and, if not successful, threatened to close all of their schools. The letter in Figure 1.7 provides the actions taken by the school district personnel.

FIGURE 1.7 Statement From Norfolk Public Schools, 1958

STATEMENT OF THE SCHOOL BOARD OF THE CITY OF NORFOLK
SEPTEMBER 19, 1958

The School Board has appealed from the rulings of the District Court under which seventeen colored children will have to be assigned to previously all white schools. Today the District Court declined to grant a suspension in the effectiveness of its ruling until the appeal can be heard on its merits. The Board will request Judge Sobeloff, Chief Judge of the Court of Appeals for the Fourth Circuit, to grant such a stay, but no appointment with Judge Sobeloff can be had before September 22, 1958. For this reason, the Board has delayed the opening of all junior and senior high schools in the City until September 29, 1958.

It is the understanding of the School Board that the following results will follow Judge Sobeloff's ruling:

(1) If the requested stay is granted, the junior and senior high schools will open on September 29 on a segregated basis as in former years.

(2) If the stay is denied by Judge Sobeloff, the School Board will have to assign the seventeen children in conformance with the District Court's rulings and Maury High School, Norview High School, Granby High School, Blair Junior High School, Northside Junior High School, and Norview Junior High School will be automatically closed.

(3) If these schools are closed, the buildings will be physically closed and there will be no necessity for any child, teacher, or administrative personnel to report to the school on the day that the rest of the high schools and junior high schools are opened.

Meanwhile all elementary schools will be opened on September 22, 1958, including any classes from the first through the sixth grade which are conducted in Willard and Norview Junior High School buildings.

Source: *Statement of the School Board of the City of Norfolk,* Courtesy of Special Collections and University Archives, Old Dominion University Libraries

Without public schools, White families needed a school setting to send their children to, and private schools, including independent and parochial schools (especially Catholic schools), were poised to absorb these families. The Arrowood Academy, like many private schools, made commitments to deny the presence of Black students in their schools. Figure 1.8 is a signed affidavit from the school principal in 1967, guaranteeing that their school remain segregated.

FIGURE 1.8 Signed Affidavit of Budget and School Segregation

AFFIDAVIT

STATE OF _VIRGINIA_,
(name)

NORFOLK OF _Frances A. Smith_, to-wit:
(City or County)   (name)

This day personally appeared before me, _Herbert L. Perlin_
(name of Notary Public)
a Notary Public in and for the City/County aforesaid, in the State aforesaid, _Frances A. Smith_, who, being by me first duly
(name of affiant)
sworn, on his/her oath says:

1. That he/she is the _Owner - directress_ of
(title)
Arrowood Academy and is duly authorized to make
(name of school)
this affidavit.

2. That the attached copy of the operating budget of _Arrowood Academy_, itemized by sources of revenue,
(name of school)
is a true copy of the operating budget of said school, and that all of the information set forth on the sheets attached hereto is true and correct for the _1965-1966_ school year to the best of his/her knowledge, information and belief;

3. That said school:

(a) accepts pupils regardless of their race or color.

(X) refuses to accept pupils on account of their race or color.
(Delete (a) or (b), whichever is not the case.)

Frances A. Smith
(Signature of affiant)

(Continued)

(Continued)

> Subscribed and sworn to before me, this 23rd day of November, 19 65. In testimony whereof I have hereunto set my hand and seal the day, month and year aforesaid.
>
> My commission expires 3-12-68.
>
> (SEAL)
>
> Notary Public

Source: *Affidavit, Frances A. Smith,* Courtesy of Special Collections and University Archives, Old Dominion University Libraries

Such examples of private schools refusing to enroll Black children also occurred simultaneously in public schools. In 1958, Virginia governor J. Lindsay Almond closed schools in Warren County, Charlottesville, and Norfolk in order to prevent Black students from attending those White schools. Prince Edward County also closed their public schools from 1959 until 1964. White students attended private schools for which they received tuition grants to attend (www.odu.edu/library/special-collections/dove/timeline). Virginia eventually began to implement methods of desegregation. Some of these methods resulted in policies that approached this issue with an equality frame rather than an equity frame. For example, in Norfolk schools they sought to create teacher staffing that mirrored the student enrollment (see Figure 1.9). However, such actions were counterintuitive in certain schools, particularly predominantly Black schools.

FIGURE 1.9   Statement From Booker T. Washington High School

File 4/10/70

> The Official Position of the Faculty of Booker T. Washington High School on the Faculty Desegregation Portion of the Norfolk School Board Plan
>
> We, the members of the faculty of Booker T. Washington High School, in full recognition of the School Board's responsibilty to wipe out all vestiges of a dual school system in the City of Norfolk, wish to register, at this time, our opposition to that portion of the Norfolk School Board Plan which requires a 78% white to 22% black teacher ratio at Booker T. Washington High School by September, 1971.

> The basis of our discontent is to be found in the uniqueness of our situation. Of the five high schools in Norfolk, Booker T. Washington is the only one with fewer than ten students of the opposite race. In other words, we have a black student body. Yet, an administrative decision has determined that we should have a majority white faculty.
>
> It is our collective opinion that a majority white faculty at Booker T. Washington is an unsound educational experiment which is destined to disrupt the instructional program and that such a fraud should not be perpetrated upon the black students or white teachers who would be assigned to this school.
>
> Even though faculty desegregation has proceeded normally at Booker T. Washington High School, we have reason to believe that the climate within the school and in the black community does not lend itself to the installation of a majority white faculty at this time.
>
> We are guided in our opinion by a series of events and decisions which have left a great deal to be desired in the minds of the black community, and this is mirrored in the thinking and actions of our students.

Source: *The Official Position of the Faculty of Booker T. Washington High School on the Faculty Desegregation Portion of the Norfolk School Board Plan*, Courtesy of Special Collections and University Archives, Old Dominion University Libraries

---

I note the historical terrain of Whiteness valuation and people of color devaluation to highlight the ways in which public and private actors managed to make agreements despite legal and regulatory requirements such as *Brown v. Board of Education*. In other words, Whiteness as an ideology was able to sustain its operation. The removal of Indigenous children and placement in "civilizing" schools, the segregation of Mexican students based on their language, and the deliberate tactics of Virginia communities to maintain segregation showcase how Whiteness and its cultural tools were utilized to reconstruct *Plessy v. Ferguson*. In fact, such agreements did not dissipate but rather spread into other educational practices to reconstruct a 20th century *Plessy v. Ferguson*. More specifically, practices such as special education and gifted/Advanced Placement (AP)/Honors enrollment and classification, as well as discipline patterns, became additional segregated spaces in which schools used Whiteness ideology to reinforce associational biases regarding cognitive and cultural superiority or inferiority.

School Segregation 70 Years Later: Laws and Policies Continue to Sustain Whiteness

Over the last 70 years, the pattern of student school enrollment has dramatically shifted from majority White to majority students of color, namely Latinx, Black, Asian, multiracial, and Native American. As noted by a 2022 Government Accountability Office (GAO) report, during the 1950s White students comprised over 90% of public school enrollment. During the 2020–2021 school year, White students comprised 46% of enrollment while the remaining 54% represented other racial and ethnic groups—28% Latinx, 15% Black, 6% Asian, 4% multiracial, and 1% Native American (U.S. GAO, 2022). Such a shift in demographics in schools creates opportunities for an expansion of cross-cultural experiences.

First, despite the overall racial and ethnic diversification of schools, White students, in particular, continue to enroll in schools with predominantly White students (U.S. GAO, 2022). Figure 1.10 demonstrates the percentage of students by race/ethnicity attending schools with 75% of students of the same race/ethnicity. Between the 2014–2015 and 2020–2021

FIGURE 1.10 Percentage of Students by Race/Ethnicity Attending School Where 75% or More of Students Are of Their Own Race/Ethnicity

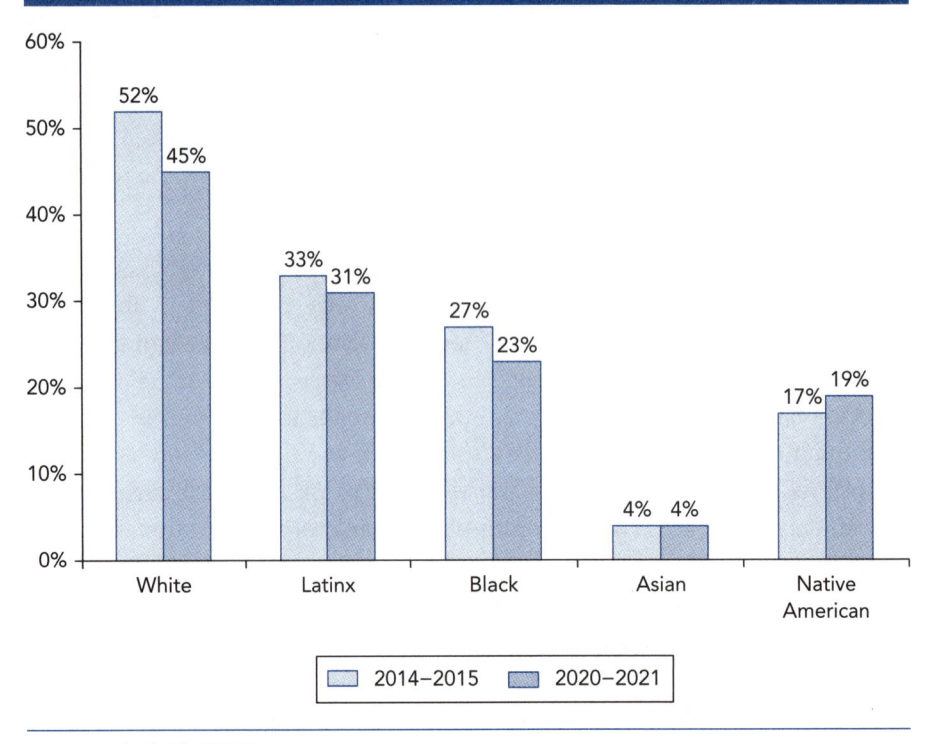

Race/Ethnicity	2014–2015	2020–2021
White	52%	45%
Latinx	33%	31%
Black	27%	23%
Asian	4%	4%
Native American	17%	19%

Source: U.S. GAO (2022).

school years, the level of school segregation decreased for all groups except Native Americans. Further layered in this pattern is that among schools with predominantly (75% or more) Black, Latinx, and Native American student enrollment, 80% largely enroll students eligible for the free or reduced-price lunch program. The concern about such patterns is twofold: (1) the external policy factors that extend these patterns and (2) the associational and affinity bias perpetuated in all schools.

Before we explore these concerns, let us understand more about these patterns of segregation. The U.S. GAO (2022) also highlights that segregation is most pronounced in the Midwest and Northeast for White students, the South for Black students, and the West for Latinx students. More specifically, of all schools in the Midwest and Northeast, 52% and 41%, respectively, have enrollment comprising 75% or more White students (U.S. GAO, 2022). In the West, of all schools, nearly 17% have enrollment comprising 75% or more Latinx students. And in the South, nearly 7% of all schools have enrollment comprising 75% or more Black students. These patterns highlight school segregation as regionally based. Additionally, the concentration of segregation by locale is the following:

- Majority of White schools are in rural areas followed by towns and suburbs.
- Majority of Latinx schools are in urban areas followed by suburbs.
- Majority of Black schools are in urban areas followed by suburbs.
- Majority of Asian schools are in suburbs.
- Majority of Native American schools are in rural areas. (U.S. GAO, 2022)

These patterns demonstrate the distribution of this segregation. However, they only showcase de facto segregation, which on the surface has no explicit exclusionary laws based on race/ethnicity. These patterns of segregation create conditions that sustain associational and affinity bias. An example of these tools in use occurs in the growing practice of communities seceding from each other. Between 2009–2010 and 2019–2020, 36 new school districts successfully seceded from existing districts (U.S. GAO, 2022) despite various levels of legal precedence, such as *Wright v. Council of City of Emporia* (1972), that continue to serve as reasoning for the limitation of secession. However, as Taylor et al. (2019) argue, "These structures and decisions use rational discourse citing race-neutral reasons or structures to further racial inequality without invoking intentional racist beliefs" (p. 3). This rational discourse is of particular interest because of its implied narrative of monopoly and fear.

For example, Shelby County, Tennessee, has created six new school districts since 2011. Shelby County encompasses Memphis City schools and surrounding suburbs. In 2008, the Shelby County school board sought a new status designation that would allow it to raise funds just for the suburb schools. Prior to receiving that special status, various taxes such as school tax were shared countywide. Given the imbalanced funding between Memphis City and the suburb communities, the suburb communities provided the greatest amount of school funding. By the 2014–2015 school year, six new, wealthier, and Whiter school districts were created. The Shelby County commissioner at the time was reported as stating, "There are a lot of problems in the inner city and big city that we don't have in municipalities in terms of poverty and crime . . . We're able to give folks more opportunities because our schools are smaller."[11] During the 1950s, 1960s, and 1970s, in the height of school desegregation, many predominantly White communities used the fear of losing as language to explicitly communicate a fear of the other group. In our current era, fear language is cloaked in notions of community safety such as crime, loss of employment, neighborhood safety, and unknown community members. Additionally, the language of monopoly is used and framed in terms of neighborhood schools, parents' rights, religious liberty, and local control. Communities in various parts of the country—the Bayou area of Louisiana, central New Jersey, Maine, Boston, and others—demonstrate ways in which Whiteness plays a role in sustaining or reconstructing schools that parallel the public school enrollment of the 1950s. Unfortunately, in our current era, parallel social movements of anti-integration disguised in fear language such as "anti-CRT" (critical race theory) and "anti-trans" furthers such actions through curriculum. Thus, fear of losing and monopoly orientations are the current fashioned strategies to employ Whiteness ideology in sustaining segregated schools.

Whiteness Ideology in School Practice: Special Education, Gifted, and Discipline

Several years ago, I visited with an elementary school principal (biracial male) to discuss his latest attempts to racially and ethnically integrate his gifted program. The district was 45% Black, 30% White, 15%

---

[11]Bauman, C. (2017, June 21). Memphis–Shelby County spotlighted in national report on school district succession. *Chalkbeat Tennessee*. https://tn.chalkbeat.org/2017/6/21/21102787/memphis-shelby-county-spotlighted-in-national-report-on-school-district-secession

Latinx, 8% Asian, and 2% Native American; however, his elementary school was 90% White, 5% Asian, and 5% Black due to a long history of housing segregation that dictated school enrollment policy, which focused on "neighborhood schools." During my visit, he shared that the prior week he met with a Black female third grader who hit another Black student. When he asked her what happened, the student shared that she felt so angry about "being Black at the school." She referenced how none of the Black kids were pulled for the enrichment gifted program, a process in which the gifted teachers went to various classes and requested the "gifted" students be pulled out and sent to the enrichment class. The principal shared this story as testimony of how this educational practice affected Black students and as justification for fixing this high-priority issue.

This story highlights the manner in which the current patterns of disparity in special education, discipline, or gifted/AP/Honors enrollment serve as evidence of the harm that occurs from these patterns. From this Black student's perspective, students experienced an associational bias developed and implemented at the school. Unfortunately, we base our orientation for how we validate programming like gifted/AP/Honors on the assumption that cognitive "gifts" are inherited or natural and based on validated assessments (both subjective and objective). Let's discuss how within the four walls of schools we use tools of validity (assessments, observation tools, etc.) to determine levels of cognitive development; however, such tools emerged from an ideology that placed White populations as the standard.

In 1869, Francis Galton, an anthropologist and geneticist, published *Hereditary Genius* in which he discussed a study of intelligence among 400 British men and concluded that intelligence was hereditary:

> The general plan of my argument is to show that high reputation is a pretty accurate test of high ability; next to discuss the relationships of a large body of fairly eminent men—namely, the Judges of England from 1660 to 1868, the Statesmen of the time of George III, and the Premiers during the last 100 years—and to obtain from these a general survey of the laws of heredity in respect to genius. Then I shall examine, in order, the kindred of the most illustrious Commanders, men of Literature and of Science, Poets, Painters, and Musicians, of whom history speaks. (p. 2)

While he originally intended for the book to explore the degree to which intelligence was hereditary via the examination of 400 British

White men, Galton also shared his opinion about Black people, especially their lack of intelligence. In fact, Galton argued that "negroes" exist in the lower-class levels he developed (i.e., a to f):

> [T]he number among the negroes of those whom we should call half-witted men is very large. Every book alluding to negro servants in America is full of instances. I was myself much impressed by this fact during my travels in Africa. The mistakes the negroes made in their own matters were so childish, stupid, and simpleton-like, as frequently to make me ashamed of my own species. I do not think it any exaggeration to say that their c is as low as our e, which would be a difference of two grades, as before. I have no information as to actual idiocy among the negroes—I mean, of course, of that class of idiocy which is not due to disease. (p. 338)

Such research, as well as work from Hollingworth (1926) and Terman (1916), in the early 20th century was representative of the concept of eugenics. Eugenics promoted the idea of identifying populations of greater intellectual stock and possibly improving a society through a genetic selection process—that is, removing populations with genetic defects. Terman (1916) described "Spanish-Indian, Mexican, and Negro":

> Their dullness seems to be racial, or at least inherent in the family stocks from which they come.... Children of this group should be segregated in special classes and be given instruction that is concrete and practical. They cannot master abstractions, but they can often be made efficient workers.... There is no possibility at present of convincing society that they should not reproduce. (pp. 91–92)

Terman specifically revamped the Stanford–Binet IQ test to measure cognitive abilities and promoted its use in military assignment and school segregation. Hollingworth (1926) similarly argued for lower cognitive capacities particularly among "negro" children and in particular using IQ tests to rationalize the segregation of children:

> Several surveys have been made to test the mentality of negro children. These surveys unexceptionally show a low average of intellect among children having negro blood. Comparatively few of these children are found within the range which includes the best one per cent of white children.

> It is, however, possible by prolonged search to find an occasional negro or mulatto child testing about 130 IQ . . . more than a mere suggestion that negro children furnish fewer gifted individuals than white children do, in the United States. (pp. 69–70)

Such eugenic notions were bound not only to race but also to socioeconomic class. Hollingworth (1926) rationalized that since the greatest number of gifted children came from "skilled" households, something about economic status engendered the development of gifted children:

> More recent and much wider investigation carried out by Terman has served only to confirm these findings. In a sample of a thousand gifted children there have occurred a few whose fathers are semi-skilled or unskilled manual laborers; so that the contribution of families at these economic levels is not absolutely nil. However, it is extremely meager; and the professional classes, who include not over two per cent of the total population, furnish over fifty per cent of the children testing in the highest one percent. (pp. 53–54)

In 1922, Hollingworth opened the Special Opportunity Class at Public School 165 in New York City, which recruited students for the longest-running longitudinal study of intelligence. And in 1925, Terman published *Genetic Studies of Genius*, and concluded that gifted students were

> (a) qualitatively different in school, (b) slightly better physically and emotionally in comparison to normal students, (c) superior in academic subjects in comparison to the average students, (d) emotionally stable, (e) most successful when education and family values were held in high regard by the family, and (f) infinitely variable in combination with the number of traits exhibited by those in the study. This is the first volume in a five-volume study spanning nearly 40 years.[12]

Educators moved to establish a system for programming children with talents and gifts. The National Association for Gifted Children

---

[12] National Association for Gifted Children. (2005). *The history of gifted and talented education.* http://people.uncw.edu/caropresoe/GiftedFoundations/EDN%20552/NAGC%20-%20History%20of%20g-t.htm

was created in 1954, the U.S. Department of Education established an Office of Gifted and Talented Education in 1974, and the U.S. Congress passed the Jacob Javits Gifted and Talented Students Education Act in 1988. These legal and policy provisions established the recognition of gifted children. However, they did not explore *whose* notions of gifted were being utilized to establish children as gifted.

Though we may argue, at times, that notions of eugenics are not explicitly prominent, the constructs of associating one group as having more cognitive capacities than another continues to be present in our educational environments. That associational bias results in a pedestrian belief that some groups have fewer individuals with advanced cognitive abilities because of their cultural or genetic qualities, also known as deficit thinking (see more in Chapter 3). Such a belief lives within the shopping carts of many educators. The concern is whether they draw on such notions when recommending students for gifted, AP, International Baccalaureate, Honors, or other accelerated programs. The ongoing reality is that our schools continue to generate the disparity data that keep feeding such "eugenics-like" beliefs: If I continuously see one group in gifted, advanced, Honors, or AP classes, that group becomes the archetype of advanced cognitive ability.

These sorts of associational biases and beliefs exist within our shopping carts of experiences as a "normalized" understanding that emerges from continuously experiencing racially, culturally, and linguistically isolated lives. In other words, the more often we see White and Asian students in gifted programming, the more we are susceptible to creating archetypes of "giftedness" based on the cultural renderings or demonstrations of those groups. Our charge is to understand and interrupt Whiteness ideology.

This chapter is intended to demonstrate the history of Whiteness ideology usage in orchestrating our school systems, specifically who we went to school with, who our families could get to know, how our school playgrounds were shared, and so on. Furthermore, the chapter explores the ways this ideology morphed over time to do other forms of segregation not in violation of the Fourteenth Amendment and *Brown v. Board*, such as seceding into a new community under the auspices of "preserving resources for their community" or creating gifted programming for those who demonstrate cognitive qualities based on assessments with a history of validation based on a eugenics frame. Overall, the history of Whiteness ideology employed in schools is long-standing. Our journey to interrupt that ideology in our shopping carts requires more than policy and laws. It requires an individual change to develop into a more cross-cultural humanity for use in the implementation of improved policies, practices, and procedures.

Chapter Reflection Questions

These reflection questions are intended to encourage unpacking and replacing of our shopping carts.

1. What is in your shopping cart about the history of Mexican Americans, Native Americans, and African Americans?

2. Given the current climate of state education departments removing the histories of Queer communities and African American, Mexican American, and Native American history, what experiences are available for you to replace this information?

3. What do you know about how gifted programs operate? Do you consider giftedness to be inherited, or can it be nurtured?

4. What are ways that you see and hear language of "fear of losing" or "monopoly" happening in your school and community? What groups are perceived as the ones to fear?

5. What are the bright spots in your journey to enhance your cross-cultural experiences?

6. What are difficult tensions in your journey to enhance your cross-cultural/experiences?

Fear of Losing the Standard

From 20th-Century Desegregation to 21st-Century Anti-Integration

> "What people actually do in relation to groups they dislike is not always related to what they think and feel about them."
> (Allport, 1954, p. 14)

When I was in college in Wisconsin in the early 1990s, I encountered White peers having cultural firsts—specifically, interacting with an Afro-Latino whose first language was Spanish. These encounters also occurred with my professors. I remember once, when I intended to major in economics, my macroeconomics professor in a lesson about economic conditions decided to use Detroit as an example. He turned to me, the only Black person in the class, and said, "Isn't that true? Economic conditions in Detroit are bleak." Though some of my White peers and I were taken aback by his question, none of us felt comfortable to challenge his associational bias. I realized then that this professor would interact with Black students in his class, but he carried a presumption that Black people come from urban centers potentially because his lived experience involved only seeing Black people in such settings. I think about this experience as a representation of Allport's (1954) opening quote; that is, this professor's associational bias about equating Black people to urban centers did not prevent him from interacting with Black students in his economics class. However, the interactions kept him in a place of superiority because his shopping cart of experiences fed him stories of Black people as inferior. As educators, we need to start understanding how Whiteness ideology frames our social understandings of "the other" as not quite meeting "the standard." In this chapter, you will have an opportunity to consider what Eduardo Bonilla-Silva (2012) calls the "Invisible Weight of Whiteness."

In other words, White identity is in a way invisibly cast as the standard; for instance, a movie that stars Black actors is a Black movie (e.g., *Boyz n the Hood* [Singleton, 1991], *Do the Right Thing* [S. Lee, 1989]), while movies starring predominantly White actors are simply movies (e.g., *Pretty Woman* [Lawton & Marshall, 1990], *The Godfather* [Puzo & Coppola, 1972], *Kramer v. Kramer* [Benton, 1979]). Thus, in this journey to unpack our shopping cart, we must consider how the invisible manner of the "standard" sustains the ideology.

Knowing That "the Standard" Is Not Culturally Universal

In 2018, I conducted a session with a school district's leadership team, consisting of the superintendent and their leadership cabinet (e.g., assistant superintendent, directors), principals, assistant principals, and lead teachers from each school—the third of five sessions using activities from Chapter 5 of my previous book, *Solving Disproportionality and Achieving Equity* (Fergus, 2016a). The room filled with energy and a sense of hopefulness as educators found themselves on the same page of understanding and working toward equitable outcomes for their students. This particular district, which served nearly 85% Black and Latinx, 5% White, 7% Asian, and 3% other (multiracial and Native American) students, maintained a persistent pattern of disproportionality: 30% of the total Black and Latinx student population were designated students with disabilities, compared with only 16% of White students and 7% of Asian students. In the gifted/Advanced Placement (AP)/Honors programs, 6% of the total Black, 3% of the total Latinx, 23% of the total White, and 32% of the total Asian student populations were enrolled in such programs.

These patterns, as the group acknowledged during the first session, reflected a systemic issue with how the teaching and administration community understood and engaged the Black and Latinx student population. For example, in the belief survey I conducted with several schools in this district, several educators noted revealing sentiments in the open-ended response to the statement, "I believe all students at my school have the capacity to learn." The responses included "Do they want to learn? That's the real question," "If only they were serious about being in school," and "I can't teach kids who don't care about others." At the time, I did not know whether these comments represented the larger teacher population, but as one principal stated, "Knowing that I may even have one teacher who thinks about my kids like that is one too many."

At the end of the session's intergroup contact activity, which included exercises to practice talking with someone different, a White female assistant principal approached me to share her sense of awe from the activity and energy to do more. "This was so eye-opening and really helps me to be a better educator. However, I can't live this conversation with my friends and family out on Long Island. They talk differently about people of color; they use stereotypes and at times the *N*-word. I don't know if I can do this work outside of school."

For this educator, the professional opportunity to understand and share that her shopping cart contains a significant set of experiences involving affinity and associational biases that limit her capacity to develop cross-cultural experiences was important; also important for this administrator was to situate "That is not me" or "I'm not like them."

As I noted in the introductory chapter, the majority of friendship circles, particularly among individuals who identify as White, are also White. The concern is that such monocultural experiences reinforce associational biases of out-group members and minimize the development of cross-cultural skills and dispositions. These types of monocultural experiences are pervasive in all our shopping carts. When I was in high school, one of my best friends, Jay, identified as Jewish. Prior to my friendship with Jay, I had no personal or curricular exposure to Judaism. Jay gave me my first lessons in Yom Kippur, Shabbat, and Rosh Hashanah. Without intentional exposure, we miss the opportunity to build a knowledge base for understanding ideas—for example, that not every person who comes from a Latin American country uses the identifier *Hispanic*, especially because of the etymology of the term, which emerged as a catch-all ethnic identifier developed in the 1970s. We miss the opportunity to understand why within the African American community Juneteenth serves as the Independence Day for African Americans. We miss the opportunity to understand why within the LGBTQIA+ community the history of the Stonewall riots as a response to police raids in the gay community is so significant. We miss the opportunity to develop the cross-cultural disposition to learn cultural nuances around various holidays (e.g., Eid, Hanukkah). We also miss the opportunity to develop the linguistic dexterity needed to hang out with multilingual individuals who can move in and out of various languages. The absence of these cross-cultural skills and dispositions obviously does not exclude an individual like this educator from becoming an administrator. However, unless a systematic strategy is devised to unpack her Long Island White-only experiences and create new experiences to replace these beliefs, children of color will continue to be targets of these monocultural experiences and their translated beliefs.

This activity, and probably others, helped this educator understand the types of experiences missing from her shopping cart. She needed to amass new knowledge about individuals beyond the racial and ethnic enclave found in some parts of Long Island, New York—knowledge that would challenge any associational bias she had about groups different from her White-identified family and friend community. What I consider important to understand about this school leader's dilemma, besides being a White school leader within a school district that predominantly enrolls Black and Brown students, is whether she is ready to challenge the experiences of Whiteness continuously topping off her shopping cart from her home community.

This educator shows us the deluge of experiences existing in all our shopping carts that construct a singular frame for determining standards and expected ways of being. Let's discuss how notions of standard are developed in a variety of arenas. For instance, in the cosmetics and hair industry, a certain standard of beauty[1] has affected women in particular. For example, in the "Good Hair" study conducted by the Perception Institute, researchers identified that, on average, White women show explicit bias toward Black women's hair; 1 in 5 Black women feel social pressure to straighten their hair for work; and, on average, White women show preference for smooth hair.

A standard of health is present as well. For example, the body mass index (BMI), used to calculate the obesity range of an individual, is based on White men. Various organizations, such as the World Health Organization, have adjusted their obesity measures in various parts of the world. The standardization of BMI based on White men affects not only the determination of obesity but also eligibility for life insurance. Without knowing it, we are continuously exposed to a society that operates based on affinity and associational biases.

Education, similar to these industries, has developed a way to position the experiences of White students as the standard for operation. The concept of standard is based on and mired with experiences of affinity and associational biases. For instance, I once did a walk-through of a hallway with a White male principal. He lamented the "change in demographics" happening in his middle school, and stated, "We have all these new Black students, but they are really loud—they don't know how to be quiet." I stopped the principal and asked him to be curious about the basis of his standard of noise, where it came from and his level of cross-cultural exposure. I shared with him that I lived in Berlin and Wiesbaden, Germany, for five years during high school. During that time period, when I traveled

---

[1]Perception Institute. (2016). *Do we have an implicit preference linked to hair?* https://perception.org/goodhair/

on public transportation, I often noticed Germans would stand very close to each other. This made me uncomfortable because my standard of physical space had been established via my monocultural experiences. I shared that example with the intention of encouraging him to show curiosity about the basis of the noise standard, most likely established via his own monocultural experiences.

For us as educators to unpack and replace our Whiteness ideology, we need to understand how the "standard" emerged as part of our curricular and instructional process, and our real struggles to replace it in our shopping carts. In another experience, I supported a school district to examine their English language arts (ELA) curriculum in Grades 6–12, which they had recently realigned. I asked to review with the district equity committee the books students would be reading in the new ELA curriculum. Our review surfaced that between Grades 6 and 12, among the nearly 40 books assigned to the students in this school district, only one book would have a Black protagonist, and only one book would have a Latinx protagonist, across these grade levels and this critical developmental phase. However, the realigned curriculum contained the curriculum committee's version of "the classics": *Adventures of Huckleberry Finn* (Twain, 1885), *Death of Salesman* (Miller, 1949), *To Kill a Mockingbird* (H. Lee, 1960), and so on. These books set and continue to set the standard of what stories matter most. After the review, I asked the superintendent, "How do you want to proceed with replacing some books?" And he responded, "What if they don't want to because they don't know the books?" The concern centered not on the underdevelopment of the social, cultural, economic, and political cognitive skills of students but rather on the adults. The fear of replacing the content in our shopping carts—in particular, the idea of changing the standard—is paralyzing.

At the core of this struggle with the contents of our shopping carts is a serious concern of whether our society desires to fundamentally challenge or expand the frame of standard. One of my favorite books is *Faces at the Bottom of the Well* by Derrick Bell (1992), a renowned legal scholar, in which he writes an allegory that involves the United States being visited by aliens who propose providing all the resources (oil, energy, etc.) necessary to exist forever in exchange for all the Black people in the country. Bell describes the conversations that happen in Congress, in town halls, and at dinner tables about how the United States grapples with this proposition. The story is captivating on many levels, but Bell challenges us to consider whether American society has or will have enough of a commitment to value all groups beyond those that identify as White, male, heterosexual, physically able, and Christian. This contemplation presents in our contemporary examples of minimal attention to Black lives lost, trans Black lives lost, and state legislations that minimize the discussion of queerness, Blackness, and immigrant status. In the prior chapter, we had an opportunity to consider the use of educational laws and policies to sustain and augment Whiteness as part of the educational purpose and regulate the standard of educational practice. In this chapter, I explore that Whiteness ideology has established ways to cultivate this standard via ideas of desirability, fear of losing resources and monopoly, social threat of "the other," and fearing loss of being the standard. Understanding these ideas allows us to unpack that the maintenance of a Whiteness-based standard limits our opportunity to grow and replace it with other cross-cultural experiences and beliefs.

Unpack 1: "The Standard" Harms Black Children

As defined in the introductory chapter, Whiteness has two major components: (1) Whiteness supports White identification and its related identities (economic, sexuality, gender expression, etc.) as *the* socially desirable identity, and (2) Whiteness denies the presence and relevance of non-White identities through subordination. Challenging the social desirability of Whiteness has been an ever-present reality in our various civil rights movements (e.g., the 1930s–1960s Reconstruction era movement and the Black Lives Matter era movement). One of the arguments made in the 1954 *Brown v. Board of Education* case was that Black children viewed White identity as more desirable and cognitively superior. In 1947, Drs. Mamie and Kenneth Clark published a psychological experiment now popularly referred to as the Doll Test. They intended for the experiment to determine how Black children identified themselves as well as their racial attitudes:

> The specific problem of this study is an analysis of the genesis and development of racial identification as a function of ego development and self-awareness in Negro children . . . Because the problem of racial identification is so definitely related to the problem of the genesis of racial attitudes in children, it was thought practicable to attempt to determine the racial attitudes or preferences of these Negro children. (K. B. Clark & Clark, 1947, p. 169)

The experiment involved a total of 253 children: 116 males and 137 females ranging in age from 3 to 7, 46 with light, 128 with medium, and 79 with dark skin color. The children represented northern and southern cities—three in Arkansas (Hot Springs, Pine Bluff, and Little Rock) and Springfield in Massachusetts. Black children were provided a White doll and a Black doll and asked the following questions:

Racial preference questions:

1. Give me the doll that you like to play with
2. Give me the doll that is a nice doll.
3. Give me the doll that looks bad.
4. Give me the doll that is a nice color.

Racial difference questions:

5. Give me the doll that looks like a White child.
6. Give me the doll that looks like a Colored child.
7. Give me the doll that looks like a Negro child.

Self-identification question:

8. Give me the doll that looks like you.

The experiment was revolutionary during this time, particularly in the field of psychology. Prior to the 1940s and 1950s, psychological research focused on what we now refer to as scientific racism, which emphasized a eugenics argument—the notion of biological or hereditary differences existing between racial groups and the use of those differences as justification to "purify" the society (McNeill, 2017). By the 1940s, a few psychology scholars were moving more toward the study of the genesis of racial prejudice.

The Clark study provided three critical findings that aid us in understanding the impact of Whiteness on Black children: (1) Among the 5- and 6-year-olds, they had a well-developed knowledge of racial difference between White and Colored, signaling absorption of racist attitudes at an early age; (2) northern and southern children maintained no difference in their knowledge of racial differences; and (3) light-, medium-, and dark-skinned children showed a preference for the White doll, a preference most pronounced among light-skinned children.

In the qualitative component of the study, Drs. Clark noted that the children spoke in simple and powerful terms about their preference for the White doll—"'cause he's pretty" or "'cause he's White" or "his feet, hands, ears, elbows, knees, and hair are clean." When it came to the rejection of the Brown doll, they used another kind of speech—"'cause he's ugly" or "'cause it don't look pretty" or "'cause him Black" or "got Black on him." These findings proved critical in the *Brown v. Board of Education* case because they affirmed that allowing Black children to get better resources and opportunities was not enough. A national strategy needed devising to fix the valuation of Whiteness over all others and the devaluation of everyone else. And, as I highlighted in Chapter 1, school segregation—the architectural design of separate schools—was predicated on the notion of Whiteness not only as better for the distribution of school resources but also as the best lens through which we should make decisions. Whiteness set and continues to set our standards for desired beauty, cognitive ability, quality schools, and so on. Whiteness frames the experiences in our shopping carts. I am always fascinated when educators in schools with a student population eligible for free or reduced-price lunch state, "My school is X% disadvantaged or free/reduced-price lunch," as if that descriptor provides a story of the schools enduring a challenging condition. Those without students eligible for free or reduced-price lunch never consider making that claim because the absence of poverty is a desirable condition.

In an 1876 speech at the Republican National Convention, Frederick Douglass framed this challenge of desiring Whiteness. He poignantly stated to an all-White audience, "What is your emancipation?"

> You say you have emancipated us. You have; and I thank you for it. You say you have enfranchised us. You have; and I thank you for it. But what is your emancipation?—what is your enfranchisement? What does it all amount to, if the black man, after having been made free by the letter of your law, is unable to exercise that freedom, and, after having been freed from the slaveholder's lash, he is to be subject to the slaveholder's shotgun? Oh! you freed us! You emancipated us! I thank you for it. But under what circumstances did you emancipate us? Under what circumstances have we obtained our freedom?[2]

---

[2]Muller, J. (2016, May 6). *Speech of Frederick Douglass at the 1876 Republican National Convention.* https://thelionofanacostia.wordpress.com/2016/05/16/speech-of-frederick-douglass-at-the-1876-republican-national-convention/

The emancipation of the desire for Whiteness has not been on the table of conversation or as a national curriculum of repair. Though an agreement on a national curriculum has not been reached, various racially, ethnically, linguistically, and sexually minoritized communities have sought their own forms of emancipation by solidifying their own valuation. Latinx, Black, and LGBTQIA+ communities have created empowerment-based organizations and media outlets that focus on rights, advocacy, and self-love, including Black Entertainment Television (BET), Univision, National Association for the Advancement of Colored People (NAACP), La Raza, Mexican American Legal Defense and Educational Fund (MALDEF), Greek sororities and fraternities, Gay, Lesbian & Straight Education Network (GLSEN), Gay and Lesbian Alliance Against Defamation (GLAAD), AIDS Coalition to Unleash Power (ACT UP), and Lambda Legal. These efforts have been monumental for marginalized communities in developing and displaying a sense of identity valuation in the face of a society that sustains habits of devaluation.

The long history of devaluation is also clear in films and movies, product representation, elected government officials, and books. The lack of Black and Brown actors in Hollywood led to the #OscarsSoWhite movement. Due to racist stereotypes evidenced in the representation on products like Aunt Jemima and Uncle Ben's, brands are slowly making changes. Governmental positions have historically been assumed by White people. It took 233 years before a Black woman served on the Supreme Court and 220 years before a Latinx woman served on the Supreme Court. Most recently, novels and textbooks that acknowledge the presence of Black, Latinx, LGBTQIA+, Native American, and Asian communities were removed from school libraries (Friedman & Johnson, 2022). In these ways, our society takes steps forward and backward. In fact, our society has not removed its grip on the valuation of Whiteness—the type of valuation that continues to place greater desire and value on the White doll. This central ingredient sits in our shopping carts, and everyone has a role in understanding and sustaining, as well as challenging and abolishing, this ingredient. To develop a national curriculum, we need to understand how this valuation of Whiteness has sat so comfortably in all our shopping carts. The remainder of this chapter will unravel how fear of losing Whiteness as the standard continues the devaluation of Blackness, Latinx-ness, Indigenous/First Peoples–ness, and Queerness.

> ### Shopping Cart Exploration Pause
>
> 1. What's your standard for student behavior (e.g., behavior, cognitive ability, personality)? Where does that come from?
>
> 2. What's your standard for a student being in advanced classes (gifted, AP, Honors, International Baccalaureate [IB])? Where does that come from?
>
> 3. What's your standard for a student receiving tiered intervention supports (e.g., behavior, cognitive ability, personality)? Where does that come from?
>
> 4. Write down the top 10 television shows, toys, and other influences that you interacted with as a child (12 and under) and teenager (13 and up). What elements of your identity can you see in these experiences (e.g., mostly TV shows with [insert identity])?

Unpack 2: "The Standard" Defines Educational Concepts and Practices

These standard experiences have been normalized within the social DNA of educational concepts like meritocracy, grit, and resilience. While these concepts may strike many readers as harmless, they have been weaponized in a manner that sustains associational biased belief systems. Meritocracy, grit, and resilience are weaponized because these concepts are derived from the experiences of White, middle-class, Christian, male, and heterosexual values. Marginalized groups are compared against the standards that originated from Whiteness (C. I. Harris, 1993; Ladson-Billings, 1994; O'Connor & Fernandez, 2006). Research studies (Black et al., 2018; Duckworth et al., 2007; Farington et al., 2012) suggest that acquiring certain "noncognitive skills" is essential to ensuring academic achievement and advancement. More specifically, the research shows that the social and emotional dimensions of development bear greatly on academic performance. These dimensions have been described as "noncognitive" because they include personal attributes such as self-regulation, impulse control, perseverance, and grit.

In my own published studies on boys of color, I have found the term *noncognitive skills* to be problematic and incongruent with the strong and ongoing relationship between social, cognitive, and behavioral factors and interaction with academic performance (Fergus et al., 2014). Furthermore, several relevant studies have found that variability in the academic performance of students of color is highly correlated with beliefs and perceptions of the social, cognitive, and behavioral supports available within the learning environment (Bandura, 1977, 1986, 1991). For example, several researchers have explored the correlation between academic performance and perceptions of racial bias, stereotype threats, and an assortment of variables related to school conditions (Carter et al., 2016; Fergus et al., 2014). Despite educators' access to such research to demonstrate the complexities of grit, perseverance, and self-regulation derived among children, their daily handling of these educational concepts does not pay attention to cultural diversity. When I worked with a district on diversifying their Honors classes in ninth grade, they used their long-standing criteria of automatically placing students with As in eighth-grade English in ninth-grade Honors English. Their use of this criteria alongside their commitment to diversification resulted in nearly 100 Black and Latinx students receiving placement in the ninth-grade Honors English classes. Within the initial two weeks of students entering the classes, the English Department chair, as well as the assistant superintendent (both White males), started receiving emails from some of the English teachers: "These kids don't have the stamina like our veteran Honors kids," "We are harming them because they are not used to being so studious," and "They are not showing the initiative like our regular students." These educators were merely espousing their own cultural understandings of "initiative," "stamina," and "studious," which for many of them had developed from the cultural exposure to only White students in their Honors and AP courses. The challenge of unpacking these educational concepts involves determining their incompleteness and the need for a more culturally evolved concept.

Even to unpack its incompleteness when our field of education so willingly consumes these incomplete educational concepts proves difficult at times. For example, the concept of grit received a boost of relevance when Duckworth et al. (2007) published a study of grit as predictive of success markers. Grit is defined as perseverance and passion for long-term goals. Researchers tested the grit scale on Ivy League graduates, West Point cadets, and spelling bee finalists. These demographic groups primarily comprised White students, and also represented specific types of cultural, economic, and political affluence. As a result of this research, grit has been weaponized as the noncognitive factor missing in the educational success of minoritized populations. In fact, various schools, and charter networks specifically, have created GRIT report cards intended to measure whether students are *getting along with others*, taking *responsibility*, showing *integrity*, and demonstrating *tenacity*. They prompt teachers to measure subjective qualities that could easily be interpreted (or misinterpreted) according to specific and unexamined personal beliefs. These qualities include whether a student "is polite" and "has good manners," whether they show "good sportsmanship," and whether they are "respectful to all adults" and "willing to take positive risks."

These educational concepts are valuable; however, the manner in which they have been used toward minoritized populations brings to question their inclusivity. In other words, are we talking about White students struggling with grit or anxiety? The day-to-day narrative of minoritized children's educational progress is framed through the lens of how much effort, focus, and care they demonstrate. The day-to-day concern about White children's educational progress, in contrast, is tied to the amount of anxiety and pressure they are exposed to that jeopardizes their progress. As educators, we need to unpack "the standard" in how we define and apply these educational concepts.

> ### Shopping Cart Evaluation Pause
>
> 1. What do you consider the strength and challenge of GRIT report cards?
> 2. In what ways does culture (language, dispositions, interactional styles, etc.) influence educational concepts like grit, self-regulation, and perseverance?
> 3. Where do these desired behaviors come from?
> 4. Why do educators desire these behaviors and not others?

Unpack 3: Monopolizing Resources to Keep the Standard

This layer of Whiteness speaks to tools used to ensure in-group members police the social and economic mechanisms of society and exclude out-group members from those mechanisms through a cultural strategy called social closure, "a dynamic process of subordination in which a dominant group, aided by the state, secures advantages by utilizing exclusionary practices to monopolize scarce resources" (Wilson, 2021, p. 2387). The concept of social closure, derived from sociological theory, provides a manner for understanding how tools like school attendance boundaries, cognitive assessments, and/or behavioral expectations (e.g., interest, grit, drive) for gifted program entry, participation in activities sponsored by the Parent-Teacher Association, sibling enrollment policies, and so on are either operationalized or co-opted by the in-group to sustain the resources for the in-group and exclude the out-group.

This type of in-group power and out-group exclusion I found in a high school with a majority (60%) of Black and Brown students. The high school had IB, AP, Honors, and general tracks, but in 2018 school leadership sought to diversify the IB track since those classes comprised less than 10% Black and Latinx students. The principal anticipated that teachers and parents would not support an explicit statement of diversity as the goal. Thus, the principal decided to frame the strategy as a class size issue. In other words, the IB courses contained fewer than 10 students while other tracks such as Honors and general had class sizes of 25–30 students.

A historical element of the school important to note is that during the 1980s, the high school added these additional accelerated programs (IB and AP) to minimize White flight. Fast-forward to 2018 when the principal shared out the strategy of creating greater class size balance. Nearly immediately after sharing this goal at an all-staff meeting in September, the principal started receiving emails from parents stating their disappointment. One parent even stated, "Adding more students who do not have the skills into IB classes will bring lesser quality and dangerous behaviors into our classes." Eventually, the strategy to diversify through class size failed, and the principal started to have town hall meetings with parents to get their input on what they desired for the school. In this example, the White families utilized their resource of complaint, already primed in this district as a constituent to "keep them happy so they don't leave." This tool helped sustain social closure within the IB classes.

In another example, a different school district partnered in an initiative with a local foundation that supported school districts' development of yearly equity plans and monitored their implementation and progress. In 2017, I was invited to attend one of the progress monitoring visits of this school district composed of nearly 8,000 students—55% White, 25% Black, 8% Latinx, 3% Asian, and 7% multiracial. The visit began with an overview of the high school's data on AP/Honors enrollment and its levels (general, college, Honors, AP, IB). This district, similar to many other districts, were sued for using this "leveling" strategy as a proxy for continuing segregation through social closure. In other words, the increase of racial and ethnic integration was met with additional levels. The high school principal started by describing their journey of moving from 10 to 5 tracks based on various levels of "rigor"—basic, general, college preparatory, Honors, Advanced Honors, Accelerated Honors, Advanced Placement, and IB. And, as been noted in previous research, tracks organize children based on ability to further expose them to differential beliefs about their cognitive and behavioral abilities (Oakes, 1985).

This school practice reflects the statement made by Judge Walter A. Huxman in 1951: "Segregation with the sanction of law, therefore, has a tendency to retard the educational and mental development of negro children and to deprive them of some of the benefits they would receive in a racial integrated school system."[3] In our current time, the sanction is made through the social and cultural monopoly of resources, a monopoly that has not dissipated since 1954!

Over the last 30 years, various communities have found ways to justify social closure by using income as a rationale for hoarding resources. This justification assuages any sense of Whiteness guilt or shame. For example, the hoarding of resources through social closure occurred in housing in the affluent Lincoln Square area of Manhattan in New York City. In 2016, a mixed-income, high-rise building in which the "poor" and "rich" residents had separate entrances, as well as separate amenities and even addresses, was opened.[4] The 55 units for the "poor" residents offered no laundry room, doorman, gym, courtyard, or river view of the Hudson. Meanwhile, the 219 units for the "rich" residents offered a gym, a movie theater, a pool, a bowling alley, an exclusive courtyard open only to them, a 24-hour doorman, and a separate entrance facing the Hudson River. This project underwent multiple levels of approval from various boards. Multiple entities considered this hoarding of resources as appropriate and aligned with their understandings of class hierarchy, which sanctioned separate but not necessarily equal entrances. Additionally, this housing project utilized monopoly of resources to sustain a valuation of Whiteness as well as contain a close-knit community for Whites.

In schools, we see this same hoarding of resources justified through concepts like "who is deserving of these resources" or "they may squander those opportunities or resources" or "as parents we earned to be able to provide for our children." For example, at an elementary school in an affluent neighborhood, parents can bid for parking signposts with placards with their names to park right in front of the school. At the same school, the immediate surrounding neighborhood holds an annual festival fundraiser with rides and animals to pet, but they stipulate it's only for residents. Another community's elementary school built a turf soccer field using tax levy dollars; this unique request was proposed and passed

---

[3] Linder, D. O. (2023). *Famous trials: Brown et al. v Board of Education of Topeka, Shawnee County, Kansas et al.* UMKC. https://www.famous-trials.com/brownvtopeka/658-brownhuxman

[4] Licea, M. (2016, January 17). "Poor door" tenants of luxury tower reveal the financial apartheid within. *New York Post.* https://nypost.com/2016/01/17/poor-door-tenants-reveal-luxury-towers-financial-apartheid/

by a school board member whose child attended the school and enjoyed soccer. Meanwhile, the elementary school on the other side of town serving the majority of students eligible for free or reduced-price lunch had a playground with uneven pavement that got closed down whenever a bad storm passed through. These types of actions are continuously occurring in all of our communities, supported through a monopoly of resources (e.g., board membership or city council roles) with a social closure for the in-group.

Unpack 4: Fear of Losing Relevance or Desirability

Another element of Whiteness is the worry of losing superiority. In 2020, during a Democratic presidential debate, Joe Biden stated that he would name a Black woman to the Supreme Court, and then in January 2022, he again declared this commitment. On numerous news outlets, in particular Fox News and Newsmax, various commentators and elected officials, such as Senators Ted Cruz, Lindsey Graham, and Marco Rubio, continuously stated that Biden used "identity politics" or that the "most qualified" should be the criteria for selection. In fact, Senator Cruz stated on the podcast *Verdict* that "Black women are, what, only 6% of the American population?" He's saying to 94% of the population, "I don't give a damn about you; you are ineligible," and goes further to outline his "most qualified" argument. "If he came and said, 'I'm going to put the best jurist on the court,' and he looked at a number of people and he ended up nominating a Black woman, he could credibly say 'OK, I'm nominating the person who's most qualified.' He's not even pretending to say that."[5]

These responses, as an example, demonstrate the manner in which, when confronted with centering another group, people show a fear of losing Whiteness as a centered frame. In the instance of the Supreme Court nominee, this move created an interruption of the associational bias of "qualified" justices equating to cultural dispositions associated with White males. Various studies have documented how this fear of losing Whiteness shows up in our schools. Donnor (2021) demonstrates through several case examples how White parents and educators find themselves fearful of losing the valuation of Whiteness. More specifically, Donnor highlights a set of Mississippi court cases in 2017 and 2018 in which a Black female high school student was denied being named class valedictorian despite having the highest grade point average (GPA), and was instead made co-valedictorian with a White female with a lower GPA.

---

[5]Verdict with Ted Cruz. (2022, January 29). *Only Black women need apply: Episode 107* [Video]. YouTube. https://youtu.be/2seoK5xAdjo

The specifics of the case include (1) the White female student's grades were inflated due to an unapproved online AP physics course, and (2) the Black female was made to repeat a course she had already passed. The Black female would have been the first Black valedictorian in the 110-year history of the high school. Donnor argues that the fear of losing valuation of Whiteness appeared as subtext in this case of a racially divided community.

Some argue that the presence and eventually election of President Barack Obama reignited a need for Whiteness valuation because of a fear of losing Whiteness. Politically and socially supported movements such as the Tea Party, "Trumpism," and "anti–critical race theory (CRT)" emerged in ways to sustain or recenter economic, political, social, and educational priorities toward Whiteness ideology. When it comes to schools, the socially and now politically and legally supported anti-CRT movement asserts itself through monopoly and fear language to move Whiteness back to center.

For example, during the 2020–2021 school year, a renewed energy emerged, which focused on limiting ideas of identity diversity in our pre-K–12 educational system. In 2021, Texas legislators and the governor passed a regulation (HB 3979) to limit the discussions of "controversial issues":

> For any social studies course in the required curriculum: A teacher may not be compelled to discuss a particular current event or widely debated and currently controversial issue of public policy or social affairs.[6]

The energy behind this law is to limit what some legislators consider the "indoctrination" of children with ideas they've codified as CRT.

Other states follow this same blueprint, which at times appears to demonstrate a White rage (C. Anderson, 2016) and/or level of racial apathy (Bobo et al., 2012). In other words, some Whites and other racial/ethnic groups find themselves "tired" of having to consider the presence of cultural diversity. In 2021, Tennessee state legislators also enacted a regulation (Section 49-6-1019) to limit instruction pertaining to race, ethnicity, class, nationality, religion, or geographic region:

> The following concepts are prohibited concepts that shall not be included or promoted in a course of instruction, curriculum, instructional program, or in supplemental

---

[6]Texas Legislature. (2021). *House Bill 3979.* https://capitol.texas.gov/tlodocs/87R/billtext/pdf/HB03979I.pdf

instructional materials: a. One (1) race or sex is inherently superior to another race or sex; b. An individual, by virtue of the individual's race or sex, is inherently privileged, racist, sexist, or oppressive, whether consciously or subconsciously; c. An individual should be discriminated against or receive adverse treatment because of the individual's race or sex; d. An individual's moral character is determined by the individual's race or sex; e. An individual, by virtue of the individual's race or sex, bears responsibility for actions committed in the past by other members of the same race or sex; f. An individual should feel discomfort, guilt, anguish, or another form of psychological distress solely because of the individual's race or sex; g. A meritocracy is inherently racist or sexist, or designed by a particular race or sex to oppress members of another race or sex; h. This state or the United States is fundamentally or irredeemably racist or sexist; i. Promoting or advocating the violent overthrow of the United States government.[7]

Moms for Liberty (www.momsforliberty.org), a nonprofit group organized around the principles of liberty and freedom as cornerstones of what children should learn, filed a complaint with the Tennessee state education commissioner in June 2021 to highlight that the second-grade curriculum contained anti-White, anti-police, and anti-firefighter imagery in books about Rosa Parks, Martin Luther King Jr., and Ruby Bridges. In specific, they complained,

> The classroom books and teacher manuals reveal both explicit and implicit Anti-American, Anti-White, and Anti-Mexican teaching. Additionally, it implies to second grade children that people of color continue to be oppressed by an oppressive "angry, vicious, scary, mean, loud, violent, [rude], and [hateful]" white population . . . and teachers that the racial injustice of the 1960s exists today.[8]

---

[7]Tennessee Legislature. (2021). *Tenn. Code Ann. § 49-6-1019*. https://www.tn.gov/content/dam/tn/education/legal/Prohibited%20Concepts%20in%20Instruction%20Rule%207.29.21%20FINAL.pdf

[8]Herald Reports. (2021, November 29). Complaint filed by local Moms for Liberty chapter rejected by state. *Williamson Herald*. https://www.williamsonherald.com/features/education/complaint-filed-by-local-moms-for-liberty-chapter-rejected-by-state/article_81146dc4-518f-11ec-9d9a-237001a4ab9f.html

This action illustrates how such a group viewed text that centered experiences of Black and Mexican Americans as a threat to the narratives of White identity. In 2022, Florida legislators included directives on employment practices as well as banning specific books. House Bill 7 prohibits employment practices that require trainings on diversity, and prohibits schools from requiring the teaching of an African American history course. These laws regulate whether individuals are allowed to develop cross-cultural competencies.

> An act relating to individual freedom; amending s. 760.10, F.S.; providing that subjecting any individual, as a condition of employment, membership, certification, licensing, credentialing, or passing an examination, to training, instruction, or any other required activity that espouses, promotes, advances, inculcates, or compels such individual to believe specified concepts constitutes discrimination based on race, color, sex, or national origin; providing construction; amending s. 1000.05, F.S.; providing that subjecting any student or employee to training or instruction that espouses, promotes, advances, inculcates, or compels such individual to believe specified concepts constitutes discrimination based on race, color, sex, or national origin; conforming provisions to changes made by the act; amending s. 1003.42, F.S.; revising requirements for required instruction on the history of African Americans; authorizing instructional personnel to facilitate discussions and use curricula to address, in an age-appropriate manner, specified topics.[9]

This bill comes on the heels of another bill that also limited any discussion of gender and sexuality diversity. House Bill 1557[10] stipulates that discussions of gender identity are not appropriate for children, specifically in Grades K–12, and parents have a right to determine when those discussions occur. The last element of parents' rights contains a provision in which parents can sue a school district if such discussions have occurred in school.

This fear of losing relevance and superiority has also been identified in the national moves to ban books. According to PEN America's 2022 report on banned books, a total of 1,145 unique books were banned across 86 school districts and 26 states, impacting nearly 2 million students

---

[9] Florida Legislature. (2022). *House Bill 7*. http://laws.flrules.org/2022/72
[10] Florida Legislature. (2022). *House Bill 1557*. https://www.flsenate.gov/Session/Bill/2022/1557/BillText/er/PDF

(Friedman & Johnson, 2022). Of particular interest are the policy drivers, similar to the ones outlined earlier; 41% of books banned are tied to policy directives from state legislation. Most importantly, the books banned are framed as representative of cross-cultural skills and knowledge that White communities, in particular, do not seek to include in their child's learning. For instance, among the 1,145 banned books, 41% have LGBTQIA+ themes or characters, 40% have themes and characters of color, and 21% have themes on race or racism. And in recent polls,[11] Americans demonstrate feeling split on whether removing books is a good thing, specifically Americans who identify as Republicans. Despite this reticence, the fear of the "other" in particular having presence in the intimate reading children do for building their cognitive and emotional development must be halted.

The combination of these particular layers of Whiteness tools—monopoly and fear—allows for a subconscious construction of a presumed social threat. Johnson and Shapiro (2003) make this point in their study of how White families describe their choices for schools and neighborhoods as bound to this notion of social threat. In other words, if I associate specific groups as being of less cultural value, I may translate their presence as a form of social threat—a perception of being exposed to criminality, of property values being decreased, of violence occurring in school environments, and of reduced academic acceleration or success in schools. As a result of this sense of "justified" social threat, Whiteness allows for rationalizing choices like where one lives and where one goes to school. We must understand that this further limits the desire to integrate—if Whiteness situates a greater value in monopolizing resources and maintains a fear of losing control because of a presumed social threat of the "other," the behavioral action is to continue the desire for a segregated environment absent of the perceived threat. This desire to sustain subconscious segregation can be inferred as the driver of our continued segregation 70 years later.

Now that we have had an opportunity to understand Whiteness as a social structure or contract, we need to unpack the specific bias-based beliefs used to sustain it, including colorblindness, deficit thinking, and poverty disciplining. The process of unpacking these beliefs, the focus of Chapters 3 and 4, provides an opportunity for individual educators to challenge the contents of their shopping carts. And Chapter 5 will provide a way in which to interrupt and replace these beliefs in our new shopping carts.

---

[11]Turner, C. (2023, June 2). Poll: Americans say teachers are underpaid, about half of Republicans oppose book bans. NPR *Morning Edition*. https://www.npr.org/2023/06/02/1177566467/poll-teachers-underpaid-republicans-book-bans

Chapter Reflection Questions

These reflection questions are intended to encourage unpacking and replacing of our shopping carts.

1. What are examples of resources being hoarded in your community?

2. What is the history of housing in your community? Is it racially/ethnically segregated? If so, how did this happen?

3. Who is in your social circle? What is the story of how you became friends?

4. What groups are discussed in your household or friend groups that need to be feared? How do you handle such discussions?

Colorblindness Belief

Ignoring Race as a Strategy for Maintaining Social Desirability

3

One of the decision points my family and I used over 20 years ago to move into our current community was a desire to find schools with a true diversity of 25% Black, Latinx, White, and Asian representation. Though each school did not maintain this distribution, especially since we live in a community that started a court-ordered desegregation in the 1990s, as parents we could find schools with a close diversity distribution to what we desired. This desire included a set of schools that allowed for my kids, biracial Pana-Ricans (half Panamanian and half Puerto Rican), to benefit from educators with exposure to this diversity. One year, when my oldest child performed in the school talent show, I talked with some of the parents I had gotten to know over the years. A White male said, "It's good to see the kids playing with each other and not paying attention to their skin color." Typically, I wouldn't respond because I am mindful of how my response might interrupt the air of racial evasion many of these parents enjoy, but that time I needed to disavow the seductive nature of racial repression or avoidance (Frankenberg, 1993). I responded by saying, "My kids don't get to live without paying attention to skin color because they're only seen through a stereotyped race lens." And then a Latinx male parent standing nearby asked, "But don't you think it's ideal to ignore race?" I said, "There is nothing wrong with a racial or ethnic identification; the stereotypes and discriminatory practices are the problem, not my kids' identity."

For many individuals, their shopping carts carry numerous experiences of how ignoring race has been vital to their social experiences. This gets displayed for many of us through euphemisms like "I treat everyone the same," "I don't see color," "I'm always seeing the individual," or "I have friends who are [any non-White, non-heterosexual, non-Christian group]." At times we also share the television shows we watch that display "the other" as a testimony to an ability to enjoy the "other" or, better yet, to see that the "other" has made progress by ignoring race. Whether that includes 1970s shows that supplied unidimensional experiences of Black or Latinx lives (e.g., *Roots* [Haley, 1977], *Chico and the Man* [Komack, 1974–1978], *Sanford and Son* [Yorkin & Lear, 1972–1977], *Good Times* [Monte & Evans, 1974–1979], *The Flip Wilson Show* [F. Wilson, 1970–1974], *What's Happening!!* [Monte, 1976–1979], *Benson* [S. Harris, 1979–1986], *That's My Mama* [Bradley & Rice, 1974–1975]), 1980s shows that provided limited expansion of Black and Latinx experiences and no Asian representation (e.g., *Gimme a Break!* [Lachman & Rosen, 1981–1987], *The Jeffersons* [Nicholl et al., 1975–1985], *The Cosby Show* [Cosby et al., 1984–1992], *Family Matters* [Bickley & Warren, 1989–1998], *227* [Banks & Boulware, 1985–1990], *Webster* [Silver, 1983–1989], *Amen* [Weinberger, 1986–1991]), or 1990s and 2000s shows that showcased further expansion of educational experiences and typical family dynamics (e.g., *A Different World* [Cosby, 1987–1993], *In Living Color* [Wayans, 1990–1994], *Living Single* [Bowser, 1993–1998], *Moesha* [Farquhar et al., 1996–2001], *Martin* [Bowman et al., 1992–1997], *Ugly Betty* [Horta, 2006–2010], *Girlfriends* [Akil, 2000–2008], *George Lopez* [Helford et al., 2002–2007], *Tyler Perry's House of Payne* [Perry, 2006–2023], *My Wife and Kids* [Reo & Wayans, 2001–2005], *Fresh Off the Boat* [Khan, 2015–2020], *The Bernie Mac Show* [Wilmore, 2001–2006]), we have all been espousing and exposed to a steady diet of colorblindness as the ideal—or, at times, the more culturally evolved—way to operate as a society.

This chapter will explore colorblindness as a bias-based belief framework that sustains viewing the world without race or ethnic identifiers as the standard. More specifically, the chapter will provide an explanation of colorblindness; its history as part of our societal lexicon, ideology, and identity for sustaining elements of Whiteness such as the standard; and 10 vignettes or examples of colorblindness in school settings.

Defining Colorblindness

During the mid-2010s, I supported a school district in upstate New York that the state education department had identified as disproportionately placing Black and Latinx students in special education. Every two months, I drove two hours north to meet with the district leadership team. On one trip, I got pulled over by the state police for speeding on the highway—on an interesting stretch where the speed limit shifted from 65 to 55 miles per hour for only 10 miles. This time I did not pay attention to the change and left the cruise control at 70. The police officer approached my window and asked whether I knew why he pulled me over. "For speeding?" I asked. After the officer collected my license, registration, and insurance card, he asked me where I was going, and I replied, "I have meetings with XX district leadership." I added that information with the hopes that any developing suspicion would dissipate. Instead, he responded, "Who do you know there?" and I replied, "Why is that relevant?" After dealing with another set of questions, the officer gave me the speeding ticket, and I went to the district office.

I shared the story once I arrived, and the White male assistant superintendent said, "I don't understand why they would ask you those questions. I never get asked those questions. And I've gotten pulled over on that part of the highway." Meanwhile, the director of special education, a White female, asked me for the ticket because she offered to call her husband, a state police officer. The assistant superintendent in particular did not have anything in his shopping cart that would allow him to consider that others might have experiences with the state police beyond his own.

At its core, colorblindness (often expressed in the phrase "I don't see color") is based on the subconscious assumption that a White social identity and experience is *the* universal racial construct, which involves viewing any other racial identities as irrelevant. For that assistant superintendent, his only view of being pulled over came through his White male lens of experience; though well intentioned, he could only interpret the incident through his lens of shopping cart experiences that did not involve being subject to someone else's associational racial bias lens. Eduardo Bonilla-Silva (2006, 2012; see also Doane & Bonilla-Silva, 2003) describes colorblindness as a form of racial ideology that emerged after the civil rights era with the following specific features: (1) believing that the best way to remove racism is to omit race, gender, and other social identities as a descriptor relevant to how we understand each other; (2) lumping people together as "people" without considering their social identities; and (3) focusing on discussing and framing the commonalities between individuals, rather than the differences.

This ideology ignores, however, that as much as we may aspire to become a "postracial" society, our life experiences and opportunities differ dramatically depending on the bodies we are born into. Moreover, colorblindness typically leads to a pattern of rationalizing racial inequality as a function of "market dynamics, naturally occurring phenomena, and Blacks' imputed cultural limitations" (Bonilla-Silva, 2006, p. 92). This ideology is used to make assertions such as "Latinxs' high poverty rates [are due] to a relaxed work ethic, or residential segregation is due to natural tendencies among groups" (Bonilla-Silva, 2006, p. 92). A colorblindness belief attributes the presence of residential segregation in urban and suburban communities to a function of home affordability and not to realtors' subtle practices and processes such as limiting home or apartment viewings (Ondrich et al., 2003), nor to common bank practices that render higher interest rates to low-income and racial/ethnic and linguistic minority groups (Fishbein & Bunce, 2001). Colorblindness beliefs appear in explanations for differential outcomes in employment practices even though numerous studies document patterns such as differential response to individuals based on race association to a name. For example, "Hunter" is more qualified for the position than "Juan" (Bertrand & Mullainathan, 2004). Similarly, research provides evidence that Black job applicants with no criminal record receive low-wage job offers at lower rates than White applicants with criminal records (Pager et al., 2009).

When our meaning-making system attributes differential outcomes to *anything* but associational biases toward race and other social identities, it prevents us from understanding how historical, political, economic, and social conditions limit access and opportunity and how such limiting conditions impact those who have been denied access, including eliciting feelings of despair, anger, frustration, and fear. These frames, as Bonilla-Silva (2006) describes, operate as cul-de-sacs that keep us from interpreting and rationalizing the world in a manner that exposes the role of social dominance and power and blinds those in the dominant group to the experience of marginalization.

Many examples support the struggle of U.S. society with understanding marginalization. We saw it in the 2009 arrest of Harvard University professor Henry Louis Gates Jr. on the porch of his home because the neighbors called the police reporting a break-in. Our national conversation included "Why didn't he just comply?," "Why did he not have his keys?," or "Couldn't he call a locksmith?" The limited experiences in the average person's shopping cart couldn't have led to any other reasoning. The average person did not have enough in their shopping cart to understand the nature of policing in neighborhoods that can include an associational bias toward racial/ethnic marginalized groups (Eberhardt et al., 2004).

We saw it in 2014 when police officers killed Eric Garner after responding to a suspicion that he sold single cigarettes. The national outcry was divided despite the gruesome video that displayed the excessive force used. Parts of our society could only wonder, "Why didn't he comply?," "He must've done something wrong; that's why he resisted," or "What is he doing in that neighborhood?"

We saw it in 2020 when as he ran through a Georgia neighborhood two random White men shot Ahmaud Arbery based on their suspicion that he was doing something other than running. Despite the existing video, the national outcry was divided again. Parts of society outwardly conveyed their colorblindness: "Why was he running in that area?," "He doesn't look like a runner," or "Why was he seen walking onto a housing construction site?" Our social psyche struggles with understanding and validating the experiences of marginalization because of these cul-de-sacs—similar to the struggles of understanding and validation found in our schools.

I conducted a school visit to review discipline referral data showing an overrepresentation of Black students. Figure 3.1, one of the office discipline referrals, provides details of the "incident" between a White female teacher and a Black male. The concern is not simply the description of "aggressive physical proximity and menacing tone" but the conversation that ensued among the group in which they framed the student as "a problem for everyone" or suggested "that hallway is very narrow and feels scary." As educators, we struggle in understanding the problem of how the absence of social experiences in our shopping carts validates marginalization and prevents us from seeing the harmful ways in which we view "othered" identities.

FIGURE 3.1 Office Discipline Referral

STATEMENT (11/9/18)

On Wednesday at 11:55 a.m., [STUDENT 1] was walking down the second-floor hallway during hall pass. As I stepped outside the art classroom #219, I witnessed [STUDENT 2] jump on [STUDENT 1's] back and knock him to the floor. I helped [STUDENT 1] up. He said he felt OK, but clearly he was upset. [STUDENT 2] ran away before I could say anything to him, so I stepped further into the hallway to ensure everyone went to class and that no further disturbances occurred. At this point, [STUDENT 3] walked very close to me and said, "Get the fuck out of my way." I was standing in the middle of the hall, but his presence was way too close. He didn't need to be that close, and it made me uncomfortable. I felt uncomfortable by his aggressive physical stance and the way he moved toward me, and his tone was menacing. That made for two episodes within a five-minute period. I became fearful for myself and for other students. That's why I sent an email to the Dean, the Assistant Principal, and the Union Rep, and that is why I am submitting this statement.

Colorblindness also surfaces in conversations among educators with statements like "The parents should do more at home," "Why can't we stop looking at each other based on color?," or "My students need to see their similarities and not focus on differences." Many well-intentioned teachers and administrators strive to build a colorblind perspective among their students because they believe that such a perspective will uplift their students. For example, educators rationalize that if Black students can successfully absorb a colorblind perspective, they will advance culturally. Educators also believe that if Spanish-speaking Latinx students successfully adopt English language skills and erase their home language, they will be more successful in schools and beyond.

Substantive research exists that exposes the presence of colorblindness in many facets of our social environments and institutions. For instance, research on colorblindness in educational practice has identified its presence among preservice and pretenure White teachers' notions of self-efficacy; in other words, teachers view their efficacy as a teacher in not seeing racial/ethnic identity (Blaisdell, 2005; Boutte et al., 2011; Gordon, 2005). Also, research on interracial workplace environments identifies the orientation of leaders as either multicultural or colorblind as a driver in the nature of connectedness between White and ethnic minority groups (Meeussen et al., 2014). In other words, the greater presence of colorblindness leadership suggests a lowered sense of connectedness with the school environment among racial/ethnic minority groups.

In the aggregate, to understand the complexity and transformation of colorblindness from the 1960s civil rights era to the 2020s Black Lives Matter era, we need to explore how it has cemented itself as an ideology and at times as an identity. For instance, colorblindness ideology exists in the same individuals who place "Black Lives Matter" lawn signs in front of their homes and simultaneously do not desire their children's school to be integrated because of internal worries of reduced "academic standards." The next section describes the emergence of these complexities in the two major components of colorblindness: removing race and legitimizing inequalities. Additionally, I explore how colorblindness has surfaced as an identity, further solidifying its permanence in our social world.

The Strategy of Removing Race

A prominent feature of colorblindness racism is ignoring race as a strategy for minimizing the presence of racism or racist behaviors. Various researchers also frame this strategy as color-evasiveness, a deliberate habit of evading discussion and social interactions that involve or even invoke any notions of race and/or ethnicity (Wilt et al., 2022). Whether colorblindness or color-evasiveness, the ideology involves a process of ignoring racial or ethnic differences, and we need to understand (1) what drives the need to ignore race, and (2) what types of behaviors our society is conditioned to use in the process of ignoring race. The need to ignore race, at times, operates from a perspective that racism is an individual act of discrimination and prejudice versus a legally sanctioned system like pre–*Brown v. Board* (1954), which used race to segregate schools (DiTomaso et al., 2003). As a result, the social frame in our shopping carts centers racism as an act of deliberate discrimination or dislike of someone versus a cultural system premised on the experience of one group in which others are seen as inferior. Whiteness-derived cultural principles like "Color shouldn't matter" or "I'm paying attention to the character of the individual" are espoused.

The lengths to which our society goes to ignore race also demonstrate its complexity. We need to understand the social and psychological moves individuals make to repress, avoid, and conceal their recognition of race. In fact, we use what Derald Wing Sue (2016) calls a politeness protocol to justify minimizing race talk. Wing Sue describes politeness as a protocol used particularly in "mixed company" that operates as a cultural etiquette tool. In this protocol, discussions of cultural phenomena such as religion, race, gender, hair products, and more should be avoided as a gesture of politeness. However, in lieu of using racial, ethnic, or linguistic descriptors, we have normalized the use of more coded language to both ignore usage of race, ethnic, or linguistic descriptors and avoid a gaze of being called "racist." H. B. Johnson and Shapiro (2003), in their study of White families' decision-making on schools and neighborhoods, demonstrated how these families used coded language to describe their rationale and avoid saying "race." White families used phrases like "good," "stay with our own type," "deteriorating," "risk of crime," "people of different values," and "more regular people" to describe the schools and neighborhoods they desired (H. B. Johnson & Shapiro, 2003). The use of such coded language is, unfortunately, representative of our Whiteness-derived cultural influences; we encode language with associational-trait biases, such as urban, gang, inner city, cultured, soft on crime, welfare, food stamps, law and order, get tough on crime, safety from crime and terrorism, drug dealer, diverse person, and so on (O'Donnell, 2020).

Ignoring race also emerges as cultural etiquette when individuals try to describe a person without use of race descriptors. For instance, at his office, my White male doctor instructed me on the nurse I needed to see about bloodwork: "She is in blue with curly hair and a colorful bracelet." I finally said, "Do you mean the Black nurse with the colorful bracelet and curly hair?" The habits to ignore race serve the purpose of allowing people to not be viewed as racially conscious, as if this would imply they are racist. We struggle as a society to be comfortably racially conscious. In a 2020 Pew Research Center survey report[1] on whether adults pay more or less attention to issues of race or racial inequality, 40% of White, 64% of Black, 39% of Hispanic, and 40% of Asian adults said they pay more attention.

This leads us to consider the possible rationale for ignoring race: impression management ("I don't want to be viewed as a racist for not saying the right thing"), racial apathy ("I am tired of talking about it or dealing with it"), or racial dehumanization (a perception of racially minoritized populations that is absent of humanity). Research highlights the presence of all these rationalizations for "ignoring race." For instance, Forman (2004) demonstrates that in social surveys Whites, in particular from the 1960s to the 2000s, have increased their aversion to identify interest in responding to questions about racial attitudes. These shifts in desire to discuss race and racism emerge in various studies (Bobo et al., 2012) and raise questions about Whites developing a sense of "racial apathy." In a recent methodological study of social survey items on colorblindness, E. C. Alexander (2018) found that White participants had a higher prevalence of nonresponse to race-related items compared to their non-White peers. Such patterns of "ignoring race" suggest that the purpose of removing race lies within a commitment and/or desire for Whites to appear unbiased.

In my own work with schools, this impression management strategy continues to reveal itself. My applied research work involves the translation of research into activities that support the unpacking and replacement of biases with cross-cultural skills. Diversity Tables (see Chapter 5 in *Solving Disproportionality and Achieving Equity* [Fergus, 2016a]), an individuating interruption activity (further discussed in Chapter 5 of this book), allows educators to understand layers of identity. In addition to asking individuals to find others who identify similarly and to discuss the unique features and misconceptions of their identity, the activity involves four rounds of finding others according to age, parents' educational achievement level, ethnicity, and race. At one training, during the ethnicity identity grouping segment, the White ethnic-identified group discussed the misconception that they are "privileged." I asked them to elaborate on what they meant and how this misconception impacted them. One member, a White male, discussed his personal story of growing up poor and

---

[1] Pew Research Center. (2020, October 5). *Black adults paying more attention to issues of racial equality than White, Hispanic, or Asian adults.* https://www.pewresearch.org/social-trends/2020/10/06/amid-national-reckoning-americans-divided-on-whether-increased-focus-on-race-will-lead-to-major-policy-change/psdt_010-06-20_race-update-6/

without privilege through much of his life until becoming a principal. I asked them to reconsider the notion of privilege as existing in different forms—gender, income, skin color, sexuality, and so on. I understood them as trying to manage impressions of themselves in dialogues about race and racism as "not about them" or "I struggled." Individuals engage in this type of impression management in an attempt to distance themselves from the proverbial "scary racist" when in fact they need to understand that our society's habit of affinity and associational bias continuously feeds us a distant and "othered" understanding of non-White, non-heterosexual, and non-Christian groups. We are a product of this condition. We can pull plenty of life experiences from our shopping carts that showcase this continuous exposure.

In four studies of cross-cultural social interactions, Apfelbaum et al. (2008) find that Whites take a "strategic" colorblindness stance to minimize the potential of others viewing them as biased. The strategy is intended to operate as "purposeful impression management" but in fact results in the avoidance behavior tactic. Black observers in the study see that behavior as indicative of greater racial prejudice. Apfelbaum et al. note that

> one practical implication of these findings for intergroup relations is straightforward: in situations where race is potentially relevant, Whites who think that avoiding race altogether will shield them from being perceived as biased should think again. (p. 930)

The strategy of ignoring race also gives permission for the denial of humanity toward Black, Brown, and Indigenous populations. Curry and Curry (2018) argue that universalizing the White perspective of the world denies the realities of death and dying for Black, Brown, and Indigenous populations, but among White populations their death and dying translates to a cause for policy reform. The opioid epidemic is one example.

> The deaths of these groups launch philosophical discussions of social injustice and spark awareness by whites, while the deaths of white people direct policy and demand outrage. Because racialized bodies are confined to inhumane living conditions that nurture violence and despair that become attributed to the savage nature of nonwhites and evidence of their inhumanity, the deaths of these dehumanized peoples are often measured against the dangers they are thought to pose to others. (Curry & Curry, 2018, p. 658)

This suggests an evolving cost of colorblindness ideology in making Black, Brown, and Indigenous populations invisible, particularly in the imagination of Whites. We can see this in the manner in which Whites do not lose social, economic, or political value by excluding racial/ethnic minority populations from their social spaces and workplaces, while racial/ethnic minoritized populations experience great loss if devoid of White friends and colleagues (DiAngelo, 2018).

Imagine the cost of colorblindness in a school environment. The research activities that I do in schools include conducting focus groups with staff and students. During a focus group with Black high school students, they shared how they felt invisible in the higher-level courses. This particular high school had a history of academic segregation; in other words, the school had created five levels of classes—general, college prep, Honors, Advanced Placement (AP), and International Baccalaureate (IB)—and the Black students hit an academic ceiling at Honors level and had limited entry into AP or IB. The Black students, who attended some of the AP classes, talked about being forced into those classes, as they said, "so the administration can feel like they are not racist." The students shared how they were rendered invisible and/or academically suspect by the teachers and other students through coded language: "I'm not going to give you extra help; everyone else works hard in here" or "You seem to struggle being in here; why don't you tell your parents to move you back to Honors?" These types of colorblindness environments impose a cost on the social, emotional, and cognitive well-being of all Black students. In other words, educators' colorblindness tactic prevents their ability to humanize the Black students' experiences of historic segregation premised on associational bias of Black inferiority. And the absence of cross-cultural experiences or skills in their shopping carts will not allow them to render the process of advanced courses as framed by Black inferiority. Thus, the cost for Black students in such a colorblindness school environment is that the coded language ("everyone works hard here," "move out of Honors," etc.) cannot be understood as maintaining the associational bias of Black inferiority.

This facet of colorblindness—ignoring race—operates pervasively in schools. School environments in which teachers ignore race deplete the social-emotional well-being of minoritized racial/ethnic groups, with implications regarding the opportunity for students of color to experience their culture as part of the school environment. Ignoring race also impacts the ability of White students to develop cross-cultural skills and dispositions.

In an ongoing study of educator perceptions of race, culture, and difference, I find this element of ignoring race as a constant in every school's shopping cart. In the following charts, I provide data from a survey project I've been conducting for the last 10 years. The project involves surveying the types of beliefs educators maintain in five areas: racial discomfort, colorblindness, deficit thinking, cultural awareness and knowledge, and poverty disciplining. The data set contains responses from nearly 1,700 educators across 10 school districts (5 urban, 4 suburban, and 1 suburban/rural). Among the total 1,700 educators, nearly 80% identified as White, 5% as Black, 10% as Latinx,[2] less than 1% as Asian, and another 4% as multiracial.

Figure 3.2 demonstrates the percentage of educators by race/ethnicity who agree or disagree with the statement "Racism would cease to exist if everyone would just forget about race and see each other as human beings." Across all ethno-racial groups, except for Asian educators,[3] the majority agrees that forgetting about race would assist in racism ceasing to exist. This statement presumes that racism exists because we think about

FIGURE 3.2 Percentage of educators by race/ethnicity who agree or disagree with the statement "Racism would cease to exist if everyone would just forget about race and see each other as human beings"

Race/Ethnicity	Disagree	Agree
White	41%	59%
Black	48%	52%
Latinx	41%	59%
Asian	100%	0%
Multiracial	47%	53%

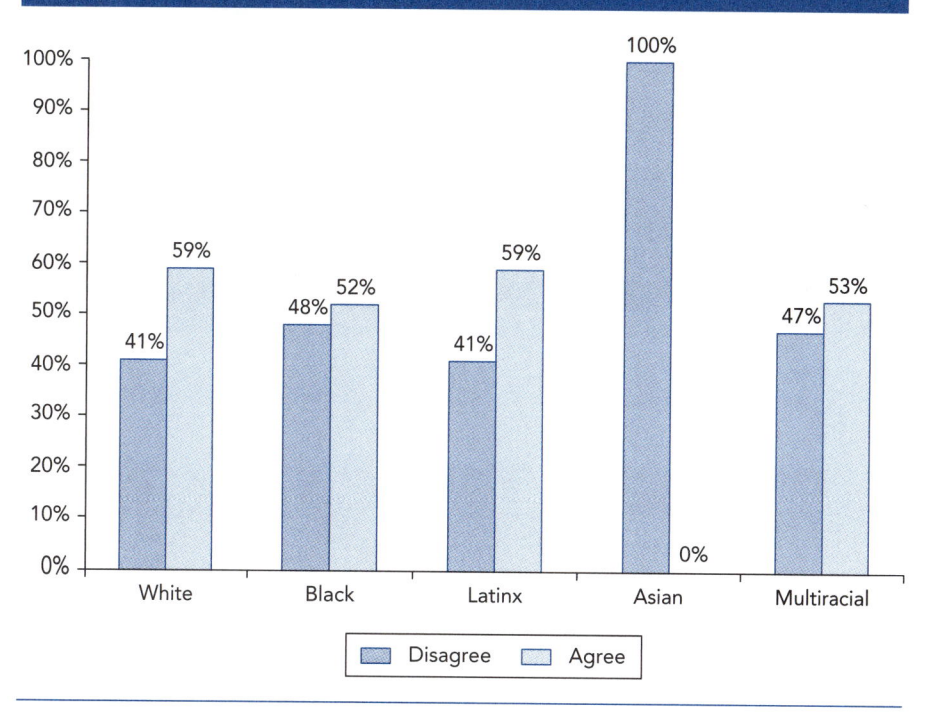

[2]The survey uses the same demographic format as the U.S. Census. As such, participants were allowed to select whether they identified as Latinx or Hispanic, as well as their racial identification. Thus, in this analysis, educators who solely selected Latinx or Hispanic and did not select any racial identification were utilized.
[3]A total of five Asian educators were reflected in this data set—a sample too small from which to make substantive interpretation.

race rather than understanding racism as a system of racial hierarchy that uses Whiteness as the superior racial category and others as inferior.

This notion of ignoring race extends to how educators view children in the classroom. As shown in Figure 3.3, the largest percentage of each group except Black educators agreed that they try not to notice a child's race or skin color in the classroom setting. This habit of ignoring race potentially means something different for each person. For instance, Whites are generally culturally immersed in notions that seeing race, and even saying a person's racial identification, is an act of racism, and thus they shun the idea of acknowledging race in the classroom. We should also consider what this means for other groups.

FIGURE 3.3 Percentage of educators by race/ethnicity who agree or disagree with the statement "I try not to notice a child's race or skin color in the classroom setting"

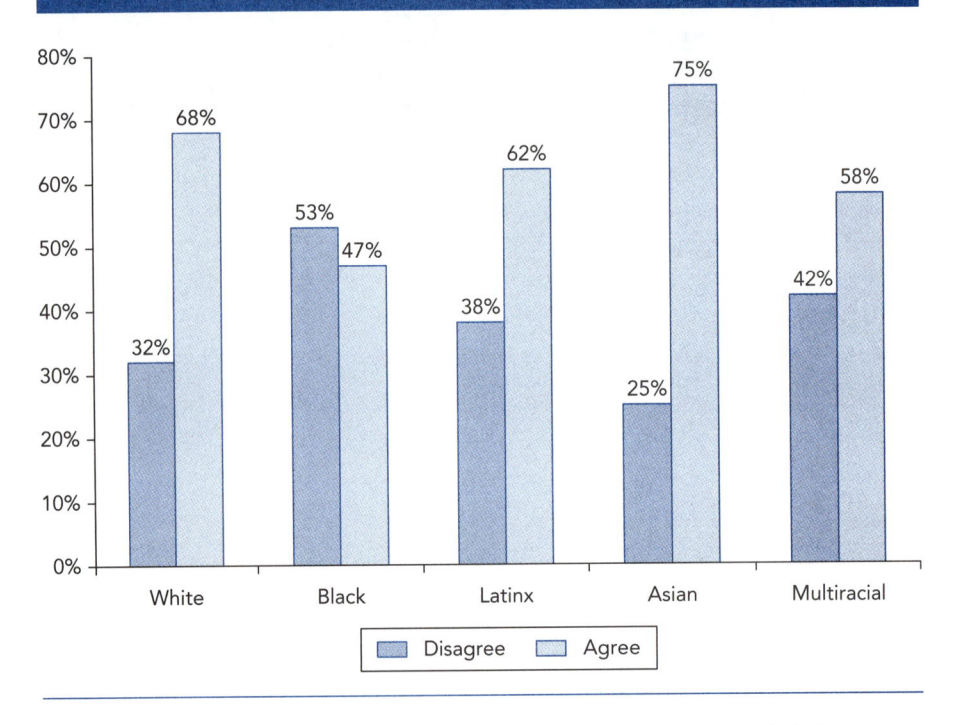

Race/Ethnicity	Disagree	Agree
White	32%	68%
Black	53%	47%
Latinx	38%	62%
Asian	25%	75%
Multiracial	42%	58%

This sentiment to not notice race or skin color is intended for seeing kids as individuals, as evidenced in Figure 3.4 showing that 50% or more of educators in every category agree. A great deal is embedded in such a notion. What is critical to understand about this idea involves the experiences these educators maintain about skin color that situate it as something to ignore. As I framed in Chapter 2, Whiteness is a prominent cultural frame for how we see, interpret, value, and experience the world, and also allows for a universalized idea that ignoring race is a more culturally evolved manner of operating. However, ignoring race allows for a dismissal of racialized experiences, particularly micro- and macroaggressions, or questioning whether those micro- and macroaggressions truly occurred (Wing Sue, 2016). In other words, by not understanding that we carry varying cultural reference points such as race, our attempt to construct a "universal" or "common" human experience will not include those cultural references. We see this happening when schools enact "universal" dress policies like no head garments. What does this mean for groups that use head garments as part of their cultural reference? In such moments, Muslim students who wear a hijab experience a cultural depletion as a result of the adults' colorblindness or evasiveness. Such a notion is prominent in the shopping carts of our various schools.

FIGURE 3.4 Percentage of educators by race/ethnicity who agree or disagree with the statement "I try to ignore skin color in order to view minority students as individuals"

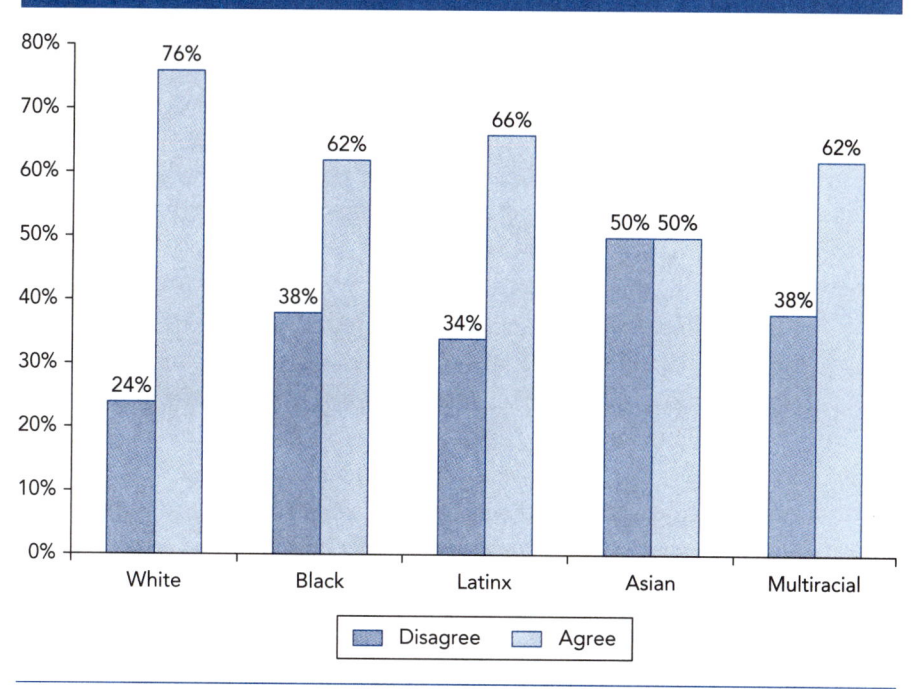

Race/Ethnicity	Disagree	Agree
White	24%	76%
Black	38%	62%
Latinx	34%	66%
Asian	50%	50%
Multiracial	38%	62%

One cultural tool used to support ignoring race is the ideal of individualism, a prominent ethos of Americana, liberty, and democracy, which relies on the presumption that the individual is allowed to exist devoid of racialization. As shown in Figure 3.5, the majority of White, Black, Latinx, and multiracial educators identify their desire to see each other as individuals. However, this desire operates differently for each cultural group. As shared in Chapter 2, Whiteness centers on a strategy in which White skin color does not have to endure racialization and instead can center its existence on individualism.

FIGURE 3.5 Percentage of educators by race/ethnicity who agree or disagree with the statement "Sometimes I wonder why we can't see each other as individuals instead of race always being an issue"

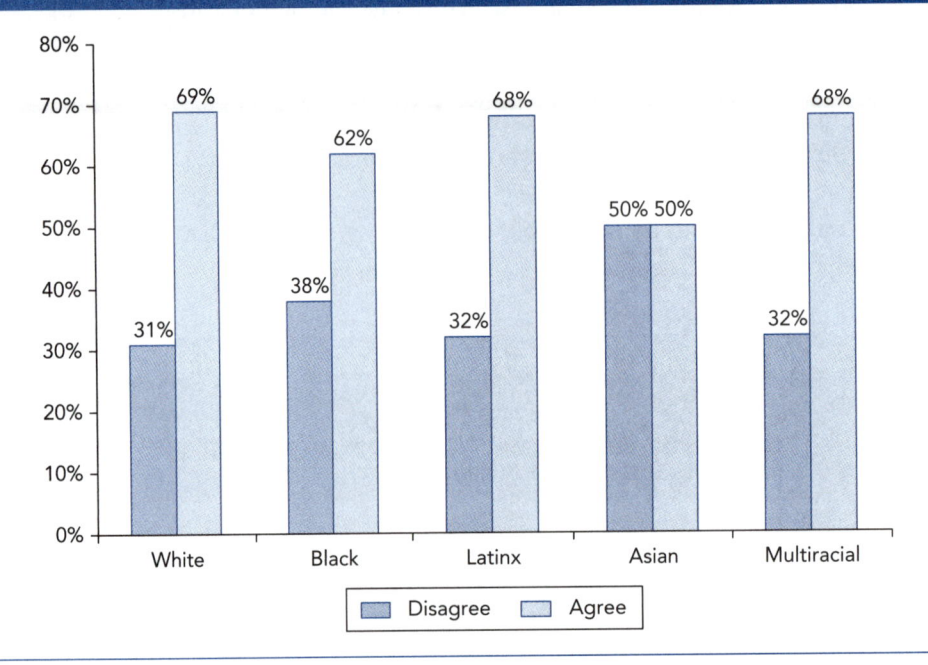

Race/Ethnicity	Disagree	Agree
White	31%	69%
Black	38%	62%
Latinx	32%	68%
Asian	50%	50%
Multiracial	32%	68%

Another dimension of ignoring race within colorblindness is the surrounding discomfort. Figure 3.6 shows that the majority of White, Black, Latinx, and multiracial educators agree that they are not hesitant to talk about race. This absence of hesitancy raises questions as to why they seek to also ignore race and wish race were not an issue. Additionally, we must recognize that the hesitancy operates differently for each group. For instance, individuals identifying as Black may not hesitate because they continuously practice race talk. Individuals who identify as White, in contrast, may not hesitate because they desire to talk about the irrelevance of race in their lives or how race should be irrelevant in the lives of others.

The beauty of understanding the contents of our shopping carts is the variation of beliefs we carry. Figure 3.7 demonstrates educators' agreement with the notion that each race has distinctive characteristics. All groups, except Asians, agree with this concept. The question concerns the understanding of these various groups about the relevance, importance, and impact that these distinctive characteristics maintain in a racialized world. In particular, what happens when groups maintain stereotypes about these characteristics?

CHAPTER 3. COLORBLINDNESS BELIEF

FIGURE 3.6 Percentage of educators by race/ethnicity who agree or disagree with the statement "I am not hesitant to talk about race for fear that someone will be offended if I say something wrong"

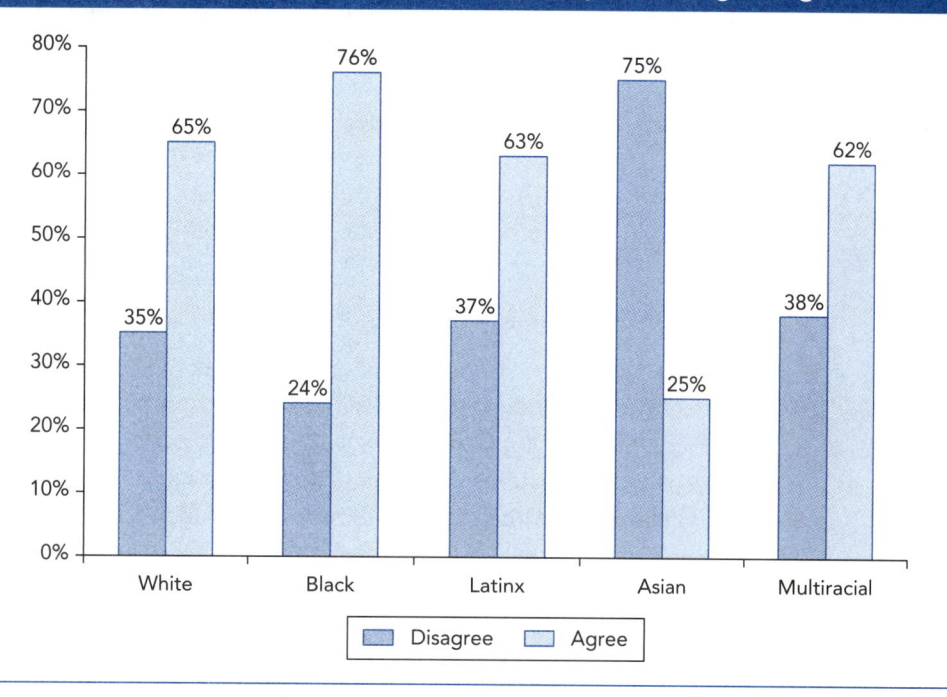

Race/Ethnicity	Disagree	Agree
White	35%	65%
Black	24%	76%
Latinx	37%	63%
Asian	75%	25%
Multiracial	38%	62%

FIGURE 3.7 Percentage of educators by race/ethnicity who agree or disagree with the statement "Each race has its own distinctive characteristics"

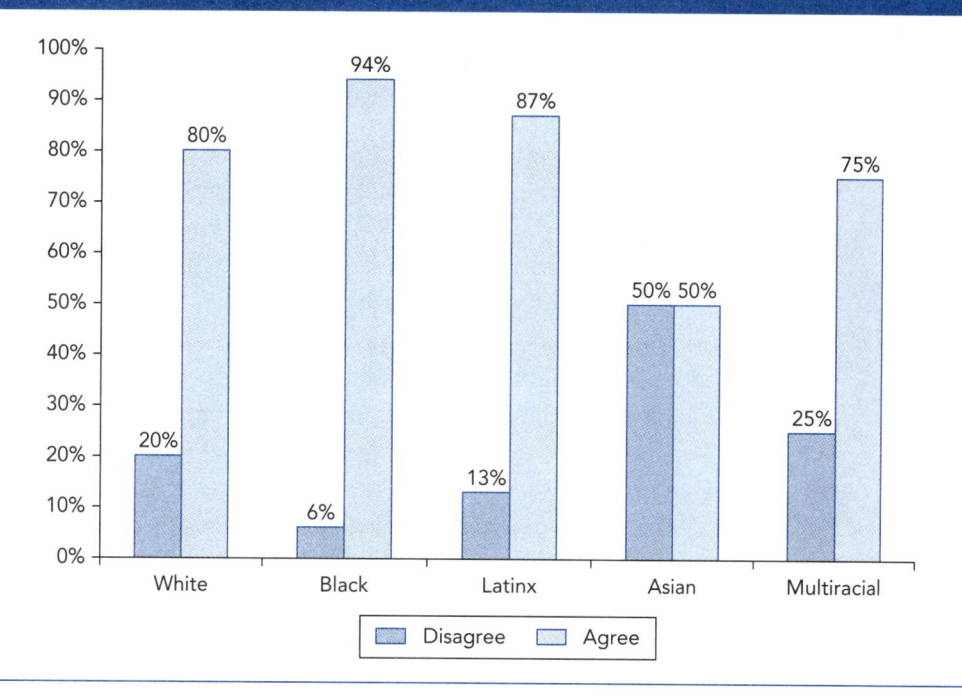

Race/Ethnicity	Disagree	Agree
White	20%	80%
Black	6%	94%
Latinx	13%	87%
Asian	50%	50%
Multiracial	25%	75%

Overall, the removal of race creates a condition for ignoring or removing the humanity of lived experiences among racial/ethnic minoritized groups. However, the conditions and lived experiences of Whites carry significant humanity, and these experiences are used to frame and rationalize public policy. Additionally, the figures showcase that all ethno-racial groups hold some facets of this dynamic. In other words, all of us carry Whiteness notions such as colorblindness in our shopping carts of experiences. Finally, the removal of race also comes at a cost for racial/ethnic minoritized populations. They experience cognitive depletion.

The Strategy of Legitimizing Inequalities

Another significant strategy of colorblindness is the orientation that inequalities occurring in society such as housing, school segregation, and academic performance gaps between White and racial/ethnic minoritized populations are rationalized or legitimized via a belief of individualism and meritocracy. More specifically, American society operates on the principle that an individual has the means and capacity to control and actualize their own fate, and this occurs within a system that operates based on meritocratic principles. Jost and Hunyady (2005) describe such dynamics as system-justifying beliefs: "legitimizing ideologies mostly have to do with differences between groups with regard to value and deservingness" (p. 259). The legitimizing of such inequities requires, to a degree, an explanation of group-based differences as connected to some form of differential value and/or unwavering commitment to individualism and meritocratic beliefs of how society operates, and how individuals "make it."

In other words, as a society we explain poverty or homelessness as due to individual behavior—"They don't work hard enough," or "They have an addiction"—and if individuals would adhere to believing in themselves or work harder or stay on the right path, they could attain success. Individualism and meritocracy serve as system-justifying beliefs for explaining why some groups are poor and others not. The result of this cognitive habit to rationalize inequities through a prism of individualism and meritocracy allows reasoning that some groups maintain individual behaviors and psychological dispositions that keep them in a state of poverty or other marginalized positions. Colorblindness as an ideology does not allow recognition of racialized systems (Fergus, 2016b). In this ideology, actually seeing race is viewed as detrimental. Minoritized groups are seen as playing the "victim card." The idea of meritocracy allows for euphemisms such as "They didn't work hard enough," "They need to put in the individual effort to make it," or "They can't expect to rely on others to do everything." These become blanket mantras for rationalizing outcomes.

Colorblindness as an Identity

An emerging dimension of colorblindness ideology is the way individuals seem to embrace it as an identity. In various social circles, individuals find themselves or others stating, "I am colorblind" or "I don't see color." This suggests not only their ascription to an ideology but an attachment to an identity of sorts. Various studies demonstrate the presence of colorblindness ideology and its identity elements (Manning et al., 2015; Oh et al., 2010). In a study using the Boundaries in the American Mosaic Survey, with a sample of 2,521 individuals, Hartmann et al. (2017) explored colorblindness "as a self-asserted identification, often proudly declared and less obviously tied to whiteness or other implicit ideologies and attachments" (p. 870). The findings highlight that (1) across racial groups, most respondents identify or see themselves as colorblind; (2) White and Latinx respondents identified as colorblind more favorably than Black respondents; (3) respondents who believe equal opportunity is operating in society are more likely to have a strong colorblind identification; (4) colorblindness ideology consisting of individualism, hard work, and meritocracy is not associated with a colorblind identification; and (5) "individuals who feel threatened by other races are associated with a lower likelihood of colorblind identification" (Hartmann et al., 2017, p. 877).

Such patterns highlight the complexity of how colorblindness continues its evolution within U.S. society. In fact, if colorblindness is emerging as an identity, then what are the implications of such an identity? Does assumption of a colorblindness identity provide credence or greater legitimacy to the ideology and its components? The implications of colorblindness as an identity are unclear, but the fact that this identity exists requires a look at how such an identity operates within policies and practices. Let's recall how policies and practices have been created in education to legitimize our social desire to segregate. What happens if we desire to ignore race and not see its impact on inequality? Do our policies and practices become even further universalized or standardized based on this ideology?

Overall, adopting colorblindness or evasiveness makes sense from a Whiteness frame: Let's remove the acknowledgment of racial categories that Whiteness uses to legitimize itself without removing the valuation of Whiteness. However, ignoring race does not legitimize the experiences and humanity of those who continue to experience the valuation of Whiteness. Whiteness is allowed to continue winning. We must take on a concerted effort to unpack the presence of colorblindness ideology and replace it with more cross-culturally bound ideologies.

The next section provides an opportunity to practice recognizing the elements of colorblindness, in order to identify the facets of colorblindness appearing in our school practice.

Colorblindness in Action: Vignettes in Our Shopping Carts

The following vignettes are provided as an opportunity to practice understanding the dimensions of colorblindness or color-evasiveness occurring in our schools. In Appendix 2, I provide a tool for self-reflection on your lived experiences and their effect on your colorblindness or color-evasiveness.

Vignette 1: Black parents need training from Asian parents to minimize disproportionality.

During a training session in which we reviewed gaps in practices that led to patterns of disproportionality in special education identification and discipline, a principal shared a difficult discussion they faced with their staff the previous week. During their data session, several staff members brought up the idea of Asian parents meeting with Black parents to talk about how to raise their kids. They shared this strategy as a way to address greater patterns of discipline, special education identification, and underrepresentation in gifted, AP, and Honors classes for Black students. The staff members considered the Asian students academically and socially "successful" in school because of a perceived cultural disposition within the Asian community as engendering academic and social engagement.

Shopping Cart Experience: This moment presents several experiences: (1) the associational bias toward Asian students, the monoculturalization of Asian communities, and the model-minoritizing of Asian cultures; and (2) the devaluing of Blackness as organized with cultural deficits. As noted earlier, colorblindness and color-evasiveness provide the contours for individuals to seek a "higher state" of cultural evolution. Unfortunately, in this vignette, despite the cultural evolution such educators may espouse for themselves, they still activated experiences in their shopping carts in which they consider Asian cultures as monoliths and the overrepresentation of such groups as "They must have a good culture." The cultural evolution in this example means using Asian communities as the "model" cultural group who, while marginalized, are presumably able to succeed. The underlying argument is that Black families can learn from Asian families' cultural habits.

Vignette 2: This is not the ghetto.

A White female principal responded to a call from a teacher to the office about a sixth-grade student cursing at her. The teacher, also White and female, wrote up a behavioral referral that described the incident. She detailed how she walked around the classroom giving feedback to all students when a Black female sixth-grade student mumbled a curse word because she did not like "my tone of feedback." The teacher asked the student to repeat what she had said. The student stood up and said, "Why you such a bitch?" After the teacher submitted the behavioral referral, the principal met with the student to discuss the incident. Later in the day, the teacher ran into the principal in the hallway, talked about how disrespectful the student acted, and then said, "I didn't sign up to teach in the ghetto." This comment needs to be contextualized with demographics of the school district, which is 78% White. Over the past five years, the district had experienced a "change in demographics" that included a small (6%) but increasing Black population.

Shopping Cart Experience: The teacher framed an associational bias that connected the child's language and race as representations of her idea of a ghetto, despite the long history of use of that term with various groups.

Vignette 3: A gifted selection process allows affinity bias.

In a review of gifted program enrollment at an elementary school, a White male principal identified a pattern of disparate enrollment. Among the total school enrollment of 300 White, 77 Black, and 100 Latinx students, 24 students were identified as gifted, which included 21 White, 1 Black, 1 Latinx, and 1 multiracial. Through further inquiry, the principal learned that the school district used the Naglieri Nonverbal Ability Test (NNAT) on second graders selected by teachers to identify students for the gifted program. When the principal asked why teachers selected particular students, the teacher union representative explained, "We have the best sense of which students are gifted."

Shopping Cart Experience: The teacher did not consider that even our pedagogical expertise is fraught with biases. In particular, given the history of gifted assessment derived from the eugenics movement and the usage of gifted programs to further segregation, gifted programming is understood as neutral because colorblindness allows for the ignoring of such racialized histories. Teachers maintain a preponderance of school experiences tainted with associational bias, especially when they continue to see White and Asian students in gifted programs.

Vignette 4: Why can't I say the *N*-word if those kids get to say it?

At a middle school with a diverse student enrollment (40% Black, 25% Latinx, 20% White, 5% Asian), a seventh-grade White female teacher led a self-developed social-emotional learning lesson on use of the *N*-word. The teacher proceeded to talk about the differences in saying the *N*-word with an *-er* versus *-a* ending, using the complete word but never saying "*N*-word." One of the Black students asked the teacher to stop and said, "You're not allowed to say that." The teacher responded, "You Black people can say it, so us White people can say it too." The Black student walked out of the class to get an administrator, a Black male, who learned about the incident and removed the teacher from the classroom.

Shopping Cart Experience: This incident highlights a misconception that emerges when you have limited cross-cultural experiences: that all cultural references are shareable. We all do not have the same latitude to consume, appropriate, and espouse cultural references not related to our own cultural affiliations.

Vignette 5: I can't invite you because you're Black.

A White kindergartener playing with a Black kindergartner mentioned to him, "I can't invite you to my party because you're Black." The Black student went home and told his parents about the incident. The next day, the parents called the school to talk with the White female principal about the incident. When she investigated, the principal found out that the White student was the child of one of the teachers. The principal talked with the parents of the Black kindergartner and shared that she knows the family and that no way are they racist. The principal said to the parents of the Black child, "What is everyone going to think of that child?"

Shopping Cart Experience: This response from the principal expresses concern about the White child being seen as racist. Here, care of the White child took on greater concern, and the principal paid less attention to the social-emotional injury that the Black child had experienced from being excluded as well as from the care given to the White child. Such an approach highlights the manner in which Whiteness desirability allows for caretaking of Whites to be of greatest importance. The care also involves impression management—that is, ensure their Whiteness is not framed as biased.

Vignette 6: I don't see what is wrong with giving them stuffed monkeys.

A White female fourth-grade teacher had received feedback from the Black female principal that she needed to build better social-emotional connections with her all-Black and -Latinx class. As a way to connect with the students, the teacher got each student a stuffed monkey for the winter holiday season. The students enjoyed the toy.

Shopping Cart Experience: In this incident, the teacher revealed the absence of cross-cultural experiences in her shopping cart. The teacher's colorblindness enabled her in ignoring the racial undertones of providing monkeys as a toy for Black and Latinx children.

Vignette 7: They need to be whipped for not standing for the national anthem.

During the national anthem, as part of a high school's opening announcements, several Latinx female students decided to remain seated rather than rise. In this district, the national anthem had historically been played in every school during the morning announcement. Some principals opted not to play it and had received backlash from parents, including social media posts belittling the principals by calling them "un-American." A White male teacher was disturbed by the Latinx students' behavior and scolded them by saying, "You should be grateful for being here and getting a free meal . . . you don't deserve to be here and need to be whipped on a post."

Shopping Cart Experience: This incident highlights what happens when you have an absence of cross-cultural experiences and perceive other groups as needing to feel grateful for their opportunity, not criticize the system. This teacher's absent understanding that other groups systematically experience inequality allowed him to draw from his shopping cart the notion that racial/ethnic minoritized groups do not appreciate the "freedoms" in the United States.

Vignette 8: White students paint their faces different colors.

Students at a predominantly White middle school with different houses decided to paint their faces the color of their house—orange, green, red, or black—to accompany a pep rally. On the day of the rally, students got ready in their classrooms only to emerge in the hallway with their painted faces—orange, green, red, or black—and when a Black female student saw White students with black face paint, she asked them to remove it. The principal intervened and conducted a restorative circle with the White students to help them understand how the activity harmed Black people. Later in the week, several staff approached the principal to express their confusion as to why it presented a problem that the White students wore blackface.

Shopping Cart Experience: In this incident, race had been ignored for so long that school staff were prevented from understanding the significance of blackface, which carried over into the students not understanding either. Also important to highlight is the cultural depletion that racial/ethnic minoritized populations experience in such school spaces.

Vignette 9: Seeking solidarity by adopting Latinx identity.

One of the activities in *Solving Disproportionality and Achieving Equity* (Fergus, 2016a) titled Diversity Tables involves learning about the multitude of identities of each individual and the benefits of developing that understanding as a cross-cultural skill. During a segment of the activity, an administrator shared that as a White woman she had always wanted to be Hispanic—so much so that in college she had tried to pledge a Latinx sorority but was denied because she was not Hispanic. The administrator shared that she didn't quite understand the denial given her love of the culture. Instead, she chose to learn Spanish. Later in her college career, she decided to minor in Spanish, and to this day the school treats her as the translator for Latinx families.

Shopping Cart Experience: This example presents another case of how ignoring race prevents understanding the histories of fraternities and sororities, which served as cultural safe spaces. Knowing about racial/ethnic minoritized groups does not mean mimicking their cultural attributes or reference points in order to absorb their identity.

Vignette 10: When not to say the *N*-word.

At the end of an equity literacy session, the union representative stood up to talk with the staff about a recent memo from the superintendent, referencing the incident shared in Vignette 4. The superintendent outlined in the memo that racial epithets are not permitted in the district. The teachers in the room asked, "Well, what can we call them, Black or African American?" Another teacher said, "I don't know what I'm allowed to say." And one teacher added, "I know what I say with my friends, but what can I say at school?"

Shopping Cart Experience: This incident highlights the limited cultural knowledge that occurs as a result of ignoring race. The staff in this incident were unable to understand the *N*-word is a racial epithet and not reflective of a racial identity.

These vignettes intend to show the possible consequences of embracing a colorblindness ideology. They illustrate the negative effects of colorblindness on students. I know you would agree that our students are the people we need to show utmost care for, and we can only do this if we truly see and understand the history and culture that informs their identities. I commend you for taking on this challenge and encourage you to keep reflecting on your own beliefs. Consider the following reflection questions. Additionally, Appendices 2 and 3 contain several activities to further your self-reflection on how colorblindness ideology operates in your life experiences. In the next chapter, we will look at two other ways we might diminish the cultural experiences of our students, through deficit thinking and poverty disciplining.

Chapter Reflection Questions

These reflection questions are intended to encourage unpacking and replacing of our shopping carts.

1. What were your thoughts on colorblindness ideology before reading this chapter? Have your ideas changed?

2. How do you experience race being made invisible in your day-to-day lived experience? How do you process those experiences?

3. How do you experience patterns of inequality in your day-to-day lived experience? How do you process those experiences?

4. Did a particular vignette stand out for you? Why?

Deficit Thinking and Poverty Disciplining

Our Societal Fixation on Poverty

As in many multilanguage households, my parents were asked in the early 1980s to only speak in English to my younger brother because his teachers deduced his phonetic struggles resulted from hearing and learning English and Spanish simultaneously. More often than not, educators perceive learning more than one language and not knowing English as a deficit—possibly more pronounced for certain languages like Spanish—to overcome. Language, similar to race, ethnicity, and sexuality, frames one's identity within the U.S. Whiteness context, with markers codified by superior and inferior elements. In the instance of multilanguage families, English is associated with White identification, thus superior, and used to create universalized frames of experience. Whiteness ideology comprises the devaluation and deficit thinking that allows us to stipulate the cultural features that we perceive as minimizing social, educational, and economic success. In other words, not speaking English and holding onto native language minimizes potential. This deficit thinking ideology lives in abundance in our shopping carts.

At its core, deficit thinking ideology explains outcomes such as academic performance as due to cultural and/or genetic deficits. In deficit thinking, not knowing English well, the inability to balance finances, the inability to delay gratification, minimal executive function skills, lack of adequate grit, and lack of a nuclear, two-parent heterosexual household represent traits that prevent progress. This belief also requires accepting the existence of culturally and/or genetically superior or ideal traits, discussed later in the chapter, based on observations of White, male, Anglo-Saxon, and heterosexual groups. Whiteness requires deficit thinking beliefs to justify the devalued characteristics and traits of marginalized populations, and to further substantiate the desirability of Whiteness.

Alongside deficit thinking ideology come poverty disciplining practices. In other words, deficit thinking ideology outlines the theory that inferior social and cultural behaviors, as well as genetics, create unsuccessful individuals, while a poverty disciplining belief rationalizes the practices used to discipline the inferior behaviors. For example, deficit thinking ideology allows for the belief that low-income BIPOC students' diction, sagging pants, and failure to track the teacher in the classroom cause their lowered performance. And deficit thinkers use poverty disciplining as a tool to remove those traits through school policies and practices like GRIT report cards, one-bracelet rules, "natural" hair color rules, strict uniform compliance, "transformation" in school suspension rooms for character redevelopment, and so on. Joe Soss and Vesla Weaver (2016) discuss that during the 1990s, social welfare programs organized around the belief that reducing specific behaviors among low-income groups would prevent their "dependency on the government." President Ronald Reagan stoked this ideology of disciplining the poor by invoking in numerous speeches the story of a Black woman in Chicago, Linda Taylor, who illegally used the welfare program as well as committed other more severe crimes. He talked about her as the "welfare queen" and also mentioned the "strapping young buck" that she supported. Reagan and others used such imagery to frame the idea that individuals in poverty need to be controlled or disciplined.

This chapter will explore deficit thinking and poverty disciplining bias belief frameworks. More specifically, the chapter will provide an explanation of deficit thinking and poverty disciplining, their history as part of our lexicon, and eight vignettes of how they operate in school settings.

Defining Deficit Thinking

Richard Valencia (1997) defines deficit thinking as an ideology used within the field of education and in schools to attribute low academic performance to deficiencies within an individual and group. Like colorblindness, a deficit ideology discounts the presence of systemic inequalities as the result of race- or class-based processes, practices, and policies. Most importantly, a deficit ideology places fault with a group for the conditions they find themselves experiencing. As Valencia states, deficit thinking ideology involves "a type of cognition that is a relatively simple and efficient means to attribute the 'cause' of human behavior" (p. xvi). According to Valencia, three paradigms support deficit thinking: (1) a genetic pathology model, (2) a culture of poverty model, and (3) a marginalization of low-income and students of color model. This third model centers the notion of racial/ethnic minoritized populations as less cognitively and behaviorally capable due to the genetic and cultural elements of the other models.

The first two models, of particular interest, describe the genesis and operation of deficit thinking. A genetic pathology model, popularized during the early 20th century, argued the "scientific" marking of hereditary or genetic traits (e.g., cranial size) determines either "superior" or "inferior" genetic traits. Supporters of this model used such thinking to justify the argument that Whites were genetically superior to Indigenous/Native Americans, Blacks, or Mexican Americans. The "science" of genetic pathology spurred the development of laws prohibiting interracial marriage in states such as California, Oklahoma, Maryland, and Louisiana until these mandates became unconstitutional in 1967 through *Loving v. Virginia* (388 U.S. 1; 87 S. Ct. 1817; 18 L. Ed. 2d 1010). Similarly, the genetic pathology model served as the rationale for national legislative actions, such as the Immigration Act of 1924, which stipulated the restriction of entry of individuals from specific countries, primarily southern and eastern Europe.

The second model, culture of poverty, argues the cultural attributes or practices often associated with individuals living in low-income conditions prevent them from assimilating and attaining social mobility within American society. Examples of these cultural deficiencies include limited attitudes and outlooks on the future, failure to internalize a strong work ethic, instant gratification behavior, lack of parent involvement in schools, low intellectual abilities, emphasis on masculinity and honor, and an aversion to honest work. Other so-called deficiencies may include early initiation to sex among children, female-headed households, fatalistic attitudes toward life, and limited interest in education (Eitzen & Baca-Zinn, 1994). This model seeks to establish a causal link between cultural attributes and socioeconomic mobility. In the inverse, with economic and social success viewed as more prevalent among White middle-class males, a confirmation/associational bias is constructed in which White middle-class, heterosexual males are seen as culturally and genetically superior. This association of income and Whiteness with upward mobility furthers the establishment of a cultural "standard."

A colleague once shared a story about reviewing discipline data with a school district leadership team. One of the categories with the greatest disparity was "disrespect." My colleague asked the group if Black and White students demonstrate disrespect in different ways. District members began to share examples of how they viewed Black students showcasing disrespect through rolling their eyes and neck and putting up their hands. Meanwhile, they described White students' disrespect behavior as looking away, putting their head down, or not responding to questions. They argued that the Black students' demonstrations of disrespect caused more problems. In this example, educators had established White norms of disrespect as the acceptable cultural standard and any other form of disrespect as culturally inferior. Despite framing disrespect as a problem, their shopping cart experiences of affinity bias provided leeway to make allowances for the disrespect shown by White students. To understand the prevalence of this deficit thinking, let's first understand how genetic and cultural trait conversations emerged in our society to explain life outcomes.

Eugenic Notions Continue to Harm Us

We first learned about eugenics in Chapter 1. "Eugenics is the scientifically erroneous and immoral theory of 'racial improvement' and 'planned breeding' which gained popularity during the early 20th century."[1] Francis Galton, an ethnologist and statistician, and cousin to Charles Darwin, coined the term. While Darwin professed notions of evolution and natural selection, Galton argued that presumed genetic markers of race and other factors were biologically fixed and improvement of a society would occur through the sterilization, isolation, and/or removal of those deemed inferior. Eugenicists worldwide believed that they could improve human beings and eliminate so-called social ills through genetics and heredity planning. Galton, as the architect of eugenics research and its movement, stipulated that selection of those with the best "qualities" would help enhance a society.

> A considerable list of qualities can easily be compiled that nearly everyone except "cranks" would take into account when picking out the best specimens of his class. It would include health, energy, ability, manliness, and courteous disposition . . . Let us for a moment suppose that the practice of eugenics should hereafter raise the average quality of our nation to that of its better moiety at the present day, and consider the gain. The general tone of domestic, social, and political life would be higher. The race as a whole would be less foolish, less frivolous, less excitable, and politically more provident than now. (Galton, 1904, pp. 46–47)

---

[1]National Human Genome Research Institute. (2022, May 18). *Eugenics and scientific racism.* https://www.genome.gov/about-genomics/fact-sheets/Eugenics-and-Scientific-Racism

Across history, people have used such scientific racism ideology to justify a myriad of atrocities around the world. In the United States specifically, this ideology supported the practice of segregation. Across more than 30 states, policy makers used eugenics to justify sterilization laws, even as recently as 1974 in Indiana.[2]

This scientific racism, though various associations and the overall scientific community have renounced elements of it, lives on in the idea that a genetically "distinct" or unique quality characterizes a group. In particular, that distinctiveness explains specific outcomes—whether academic prowess, criminality, or intelligence.

In 2009, I conducted an initial session with a rural/suburban school district cited for an overrepresentation of Black students in special education. The special education director commented, "It's a whole family that is disabled." Taken aback by the director's comment, I asked for clarification. They proceeded to describe how a set of three Black families moved into town in the previous years to live close to a family member incarcerated at the nearby prison. The director described how the kids demonstrated a great deal of "problems" that markedly distinguished them from the students in their community. I followed up with the question, "Are there other families in which more than one child has a disability?" They couldn't answer the question, but this prompted consideration of the root of their underlying belief: whether the members of the family or whether Black people had a genetic deficiency. I also recognized that the director's attempt to frame the problem as a family genetic deficiency intended to minimize the notion that it centered on race when, in fact, her framing the problem as genetic was peppered with social ideas of race and class. For this director, the compilation of this information (family units, convicted family member, and perhaps their race) resulted in the development of an associational bias.

The notion of genetic or hereditary elements existing within family units has not lost traction in schools. One could argue that schools use practices such as disability identification to "improve the race." Various research highlights that educators at times use data and research to reify the associational bias within eugenics (Lasater et al., 2021). Lasater and colleagues (2021) argue that at times educators profess deficit thinking during data sessions focused on student accountability measures. Under such organizational conditions, educators may rely on deficit thoughts such as genetic or hereditary notions to explain data patterns; for example, "the

---

[2]Kaelber, L. (2009). *Eugenics: Compulsory sterilization in 50 American states*. University of Vermont. https://www.uvm.edu/~lkaelber/eugenics/

family has problems," "see with this lots of kids from that area," etc. I argue these thoughts already fill the shopping carts of educators, and specific dynamics of school organization may allow for the utilization of such notions. As such, I believe that as educators we need to interrupt the ways in which talk around genetics happens in our school practice.

Cultural Deficit Notions Continue to Harm Us

In the winter of 2021, I visited my parents in their gated 55+ community. I find such communities very unique, with residents at a similar stage in their lives, all interested in downsizing, slowing down, or improving their mental and physical health. During this particular visit, I joined a community walk at 7:30 a.m., involving various community members walking the trails in the gated community. I find that whenever I mention I live in New York, people customarily follow with "Wow, I remember when I visited" or "It is such an active city." This time, John, one of the individuals on this walk, said, "How do you survive through all the violence?" I deduced that this question stemmed from a steady diet of specific television networks that continuously peddle ideas of rampant violence in New York City. As I always try to come back to facts and information, I replied, "There is no per capita difference in violence than here in your city." John continued, "But the violence is really with certain people—the Blacks, the poor." I couldn't hear much after "the Blacks" because of the triggering language. However, as I reflected later, John held very specific cultural deficit notions about "the Blacks." I theorize that if I had pushed further, John would probably have revealed an assumption of criminality that prevents progress among "the Blacks."

The notion of cultural deficits makes up a significant component of deficit thinking. Deficit thinkers view certain groups as developing or maintaining culturally deficient qualities that keep them in poverty, particularly over time. Then, they pass such characteristics on from one generation to another, which makes it difficult for individuals to escape poverty. This critical component of cultural deficiency outlines the cyclical impact of the deficiencies. Moreover, these qualities are seen as impeding mobility now that many legal barriers to social mobility have been struck down. The difficulty with this understanding of culture in relation to poverty lies in its treatment of culture as static and as a cause of the status of poverty. No consideration is given to the cultural elements that exist within poverty conditions, and possibly occur as a way to manage the impact of poverty on progress. "The greatest barrier to middle-class status among the poor is sustained material deprivation itself" (Small et al., 2010, p. 9).

Overall, the term *cultural deficiency*, used in various fields, has operated in the lexicon of academic discourse since the mid-1900s. Some sociologists and cultural anthropologists have utilized the discourse of cultural deficiency within analyses of limited social mobility (Heller, 1966; O. Lewis, 1961). The emergence of cultural deficiency *in* education involved its use to explain the difference in academic attainment among racial/ethnic groups, as well as a justification for separate schools pre-1960s. For example, during the 1920s to 1940s, schools tested Mexican American students for intellectual abilities in order to substantiate separate classrooms (Blanton, 2003). Cultural deficiency maintains that the low academic performance of Latinx students is a consequence of their deficient cultural practices (Bloom et al., 1965; Heller, 1966; O. Lewis, 1961). This argument posits that familial and community practices suppress the development of low-income minority children's linguistic, cognitive, and affective skills necessary for successful school functioning. For example, according to Heller (1966), the cultural practices of Mexican American families focused on values not conducive to social mobility in the United States. Heller asserted that "this type of upbringing creates stumbling blocks to future advancement by stressing values that hinder mobility—family ties, honor, masculinity, and living in the present—and by neglecting the values that are conducive to it—achievement, independence, and deferred gratification" (pp. 34–35).

Other proponents of cultural deficiency assert that this form of cultural socialization is perpetuated from one generation to the next. Oscar Lewis (1961) claimed that low-income Mexicans and Puerto Ricans self-perpetuate a culture of poverty that includes violence, an inability to defer gratification, and political apathy. These cultural practices, according to Lewis, are embedded in the behavior of low-income Mexicans and Puerto Ricans by the time they are 6 or 7 years old and continue even if the economic status of the community improves. This implies that these behaviors and cultural practices impede academic success.

Within education, some use cultural deficiency arguments to explain why differences in academic performance exist and persist among racial/ethnic minoritized groups. Too often in data team meetings, Professional Learning Community (PLC) meetings, grade-level or content meetings, and faculty meetings, when data regarding student progress is disaggregated by a demographic category, some form of cultural deficiency enters the room. Sometimes it appears in the form of what I like to call innocent inquiry—"I wonder, if the family had been with us from kindergarten, would their child be doing better?"—or the "find an expert" inquiry—"This student really needs an expert to work with them." No matter the term used (*cultural deficiency, culture of poverty,* or *culture of deprivation*), the idea implies that poor people and racial/ethnic minority groups lack cultural characteristics conducive for social and economic mobility.

A subset of these genetic and cultural deficit arguments involves another belief that espouses the need for disciplining behaviors out of a group. In my work, I frame this belief as poverty disciplining. Not only do some see cultural deficits in a group; they also believe that they need to discipline these cultural deficits.

Poverty Disciplining Belief

The poverty disciplining belief has received somewhat less attention from equity advocates but appears to be prevalent in schools and quite harmful to many students. A poverty disciplining belief centers on the assumption that poverty itself is a kind of "culture," characterized by dysfunctional behaviors that prevent success in school and require disciplining (Fergus, 2016a, 2016b). In effect, it pathologizes children who live (or whose parents lived) in low-income communities. And while it doesn't focus on race per se, proponents of this belief often use it as a proxy for and to justify racial disparities in disciplinary referrals, achievement, and enrollment in gifted, Advanced Placement, and Honors courses, as well as to justify harsh punishments for "disobedience," "disorderly conduct," or "disrespect."

By way of illustration, consider my meeting with a superintendent whose district, according to my analysis, gave disproportionate numbers of suspensions and disciplinary referrals to Black students. As I explained to the superintendent, the local data supported a robust body of previous research showing that educators tend to single out Black students, whatever their free/reduced-price lunch status, much more often than White students for such punishments (Skiba et al., 2002), suggesting an underlying racial bias on the part of some teachers and administrators. He argued that such disparities don't necessarily imply bias, as he showed me a spreadsheet he had compiled. "I'm a former math teacher," he said, "so I feel very comfortable doing relative risk ratios." His data revealed the same pattern as mine: In his district, rates of suspension were significantly higher for Black students, independent of free/reduced-price lunch status, which many educators use as signaling family income but in fact very loosely approximates income. However, he offered a very different explanation: "See, these kids are poor, and do you understand how poor kids behave? They have their pants sagging, use inappropriate language, and just don't care about school."

In that moment, the superintendent provided a clear window into his beliefs about poverty as a trait that develops cultural characteristics of maneuvering in the world. As he saw it, (1) whatever their family income level, Black kids are "poor"; (2) poor kids behave in dysfunctional ways; and (3) suspensions and disciplinary referrals can help correct such behaviors. In short, the superintendent assumed that individuals from historically low-income communities are prone to specific mannerisms, speech patterns, and actions that prevent their success in school and society (Soss et al., 2011) and are best controlled by way of punishment.

In their book *Disciplining the Poor* (2011), Joe Soss and colleagues explain that over a period of 20 or so years (1990s and 2000s), the notion that low-income individuals' "civic incorporation can be achieved only by forcing the poor to confront a more demanding and appropriate 'operational definition of citizenship'" (p. 5) has dominated social welfare policy (beginning with the Welfare-to-Work programs of the 1990s). In other words, many policy makers assume that the best way to help people escape poverty is to *discipline* them. If they cannot succeed in school, hold down a job, stay sober, save money, and otherwise behave as good citizens, it isn't because they lack opportunities, supports, and resources. Rather, the theory goes, it's because their community has instilled in them certain behavioral and psychological dispositions that prevent them from helping *themselves.*

During the late 2010s, various school districts and schools demonstrated this habit of poverty disciplining. Figures 4.1 and 4.2 represent letters distributed in two different communities. Figure 4.1 represents a letter distributed by a high school principal to students' parents in which she shared her new required dress code for the parents—not the students—to adhere to. And Figure 4.2 represents a letter from a school district to parents about their children's lunch dues owed and that, because of their noncompliance, the school district would report the parents to local authorities. In both instances, educators espouse their poverty disciplining belief and feel justified in sustaining such a belief.

FIGURE 4.1 Letter concerning a new required dress code

Benjamin Franklin High School

[ADDRESS REDACTED]

[CITY REDACTED], Texas

[NAME REDACTED], Principal

March 15, 2019

Dear Franklin Parents and Guests,

Beginning next week, Benjamin Franklin High School will be enforcing new guidelines meant to help our children understand what attire is most appropriate when applying for a job, entering a building, going somewhere, or visiting someone outside the comfort of home. We will enforce these guidelines on a daily basis during the school week, Monday through Friday, and on weekends if events are held outside typical school hours. We are preparing our children for the future, and it all begins here. Therefore, please be aware of the following rules and restrictions, which will go into effect on Monday, March 18, 2019:

- Satin caps, bonnets, and other hats are strictly prohibited within the building and are strongly discouraged on the premises. Shower caps are also forbidden.
- Hair rollers are similarly forbidden.
- Pajamas of any kind are forbidden. House shoes and any other attire that might be considered part of your pajamas, underwear, or home setting wear will not be allowed. *This includes flannel pajamas.*
- Jeans with tears in them, especially if they show lots of skin, will not be permitted. This includes jeans with tears around your buttocks and down the backs of your legs.
- Leggings that reveal uncovered skin are NOT permitted.
- Short-cut shorts that are up to your buttocks are NOT permitted.
- Daisy Dukes and other "low rider" shorts are NOT permitted.
- Dresses or skirts that are up to your buttocks are NOT permitted. They should be at knee length or lower to be considered acceptable.
- Any other attire that might be considered unacceptable for the school setting is NOT permitted.

Please understand that if you break our school rules and policies regarding dress code, you will not be allowed on the premises or within the building until you return in the appropriate attire. Parents, we value you and your child's education. You are your child's first teacher, and you MUST have high standards for their sake. We are preparing your child for success and a prosperous adulthood. They need to know what is appropriate and inappropriate in public. Furthermore, this is a *professional education environment* where we stress what is correct and incorrect. This is why we ask that you value and follow the rules of the school environment as a parent.

This guideline will apply to any and all events inside or outside of Benjamin Franklin High School so long as the event is on our premises. Thank you for understanding and being a partner in your child's education. If you have any questions, please contact **[NAME AND CONTACT INFORMATION REDACTED]**.

Sincerely,

[NAME REDACTED], Principal

FIGURE 4.2   Letter concerning children's lunch dues

> Green Valley East School District
> [ADDRESS REDACTED], Pennsylvania
> [PHONE NUMBER REDACTED]
>
> Dear Parent/Guardian,
>
> This letter is to inform you that your child _____ has been purchasing breakfast and/or lunch at _____ School. After review of our records, there is a negative balance of $_____ on your child's account.
>
> At this time, multiple letters have been sent home with your child, but no payments have been made. Your child has been sent to school every day without money or food to eat at breakfast and/or lunch. This failure to provide proper nutrition can result in your being sent to Dependency Court for neglect. If you are sent to Dependency Court, losing custody of your child is a possibility, and your child may be placed in foster care. To view your child's account, please visit our [WEB ADDRESS REDACTED] "Parent Portal." There you can find your child's purchase history and balance information.
>
> We ask that you remit payment as soon as possible to avoid being reported to the authorities. If needed, Free and Reduced applications can be completed at any time during the school year, but only if you have yet to fill out an application or if your financial situation has changed.
>
> Sincerely,
>
> [NAME REDACTED]
>
> Director of Federal Programs
>
> Green Valley East School District

The belief that poor people need discipline rests, in turn, on a highly debatable premise: the idea that the economic status of a community determines the value of its cultural practices. The poorer the community, the more impoverished and dysfunctional its culture; the richer the community, the more culturally refined it must be. Increasingly,

I've found some educators frame their assumptions about poor and minority children in terms borrowed from the biological and cognitive sciences, especially research into the effects of long-term exposure to lead paint, food insecurity, violence, and other environmental dangers and a lack of exposure to certain positive influences, such as frequent reading time at home. A prime example of the latter relates to Hart and Risley's well-known 1995 study of vocabulary development that found middle-income preschool-age children were exposed, at home, to 30 million more words, on average, than their low-income peers. In fact, more recent research suggests that the Hart and Risley study neglected to account for words spoken by multiple caregivers and bystanders, which led them to significantly underestimate the number of words heard by kids from low-income families (Sperry et al., 2018). Still, though, the study is often cited as evidence of a cultural deficiency. If many poor kids arrive at school already behind in literacy development, then the blame must lie with the low-income community's *values* and *cultural practices* because their language use is presumed to be a choice.

Similarly, in recent years we have seen an explosion of research into the effects of childhood trauma, and many educators have become aware that prolonged exposure to traumatic events—which tends to be somewhat more prevalent in low-income communities—is a leading contributor to various risky behaviors and negative health outcomes later in adulthood (Anda et al., 2008; Felitti et al., 1998). Unfortunately, however, educators sometimes interpret this to classify childhood poverty *itself* as a form of trauma.

Countless times, I've heard practitioners use the phrase "trauma kids" to describe students with eligibility for free/reduced-price lunch. And in some instances, school practitioners even go so far as to argue that students' low-income status alone justifies their placement in special education or remedial academic services. Recently, for example, when I visited a school to review its tiered approach to providing social and emotional supports, the principal shared with me their interpretation of a trauma-informed workshop they had attended. Referring to kids growing up in poverty, the principal noted that "the research shows that the frontal lobe of their brain is being activated during their fight or flight mode and causes them to have smaller brains in the back of their head. . . . I think these kids need to be placed in a self-contained environment so they can get the necessary support."

In short, not only do significant numbers of educators believe that when students from low-income backgrounds struggle it must be the fault of their culture, but some educators dress up that belief in "scientific" evidence about growing up in poverty. Supposedly, the nature of low-income families is to expose their children to trauma and to deny them appropriate support for language development.

But in fact, mountains of research findings suggest that while poverty may put children at a somewhat elevated risk for trauma and other negative influences on development, poverty is far from a deterministic condition (Spencer, 2006). An individual student has trouble learning to read, behaving appropriately in class, or meeting other expectations for complex reasons related to that individual and the people and institutions in their lives, not simply *because* they are poor.

Genetic and Cultural Deficit Thinking Present in Our Schools

In the following charts, I provide data from the survey project I've been conducting for the last 10 years. Deficit thinking involves the presumption of abilities bound to low-income conditions. Figure 4.3 demonstrates the percentage of educators who agree or disagree that "disadvantaged students generally do not have the abilities necessary to succeed in the classroom." The majority of educators disagree with this

FIGURE 4.3 The percentage of educators by race/ethnicity who agree or disagree with the statement "Disadvantaged students generally do not have the abilities necessary to succeed in the classroom"

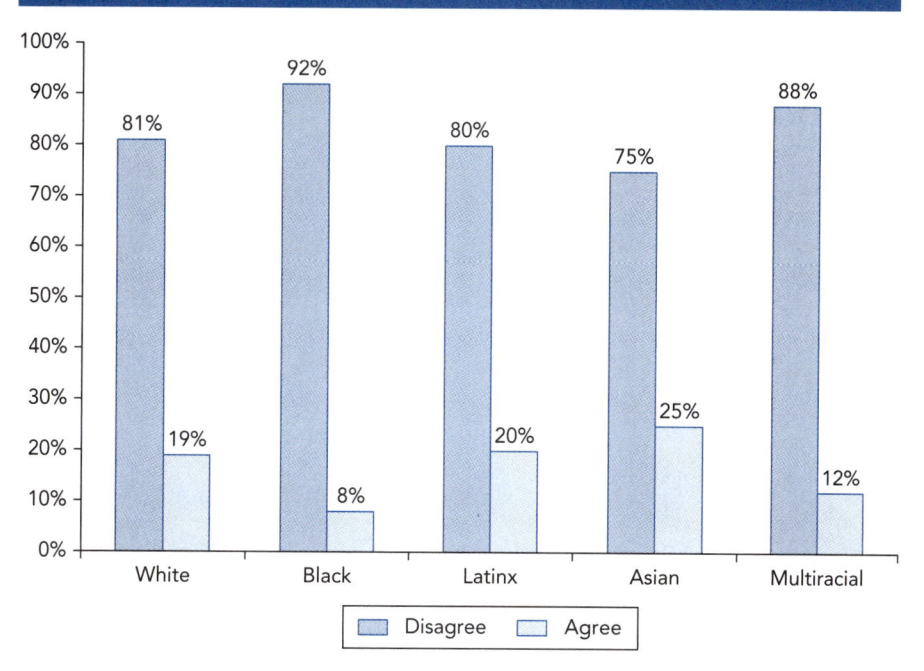

Race/Ethnicity	Disagree	Agree
White	81%	19%
Black	92%	8%
Latinx	80%	20%
Asian	75%	25%
Multiracial	88%	12%

deficit frame. However, within each group of educators, except Black, nearly 20% agree. This suggests that about 20% of educators believe that disadvantaged students lack the abilities to succeed in school. Educators probably consider a range of attributes explanatory for why educational success cannot occur unless these attributes improve.

Figure 4.4 further expands the belief educators maintain about the capacities of students from disadvantaging conditions. The majority of educators in each group disagree with the belief that students from such conditions do not value education. Of concern, again, is the nature to which 16% to 30% of educators agree with this deficit notion, especially the 30% of White educators who agree. This particular belief centers on the idea that valuing education is a significant element of success. When I ask educators to describe examples of students not valuing education, they say "They show up late," "They can never turn in homework on time," or "We can't always give them second and third chances; that's not how real life works." The educators presume that these cultural traits limit these students' progress while romanticizing that such habits exist among affluent, advantaged students and are the rationale for their success. Unfortunately, such a

FIGURE 4.4 The percentage of educators by race/ethnicity who agree or disagree with the statement "Students from disadvantaged backgrounds do not value education as much as other students"

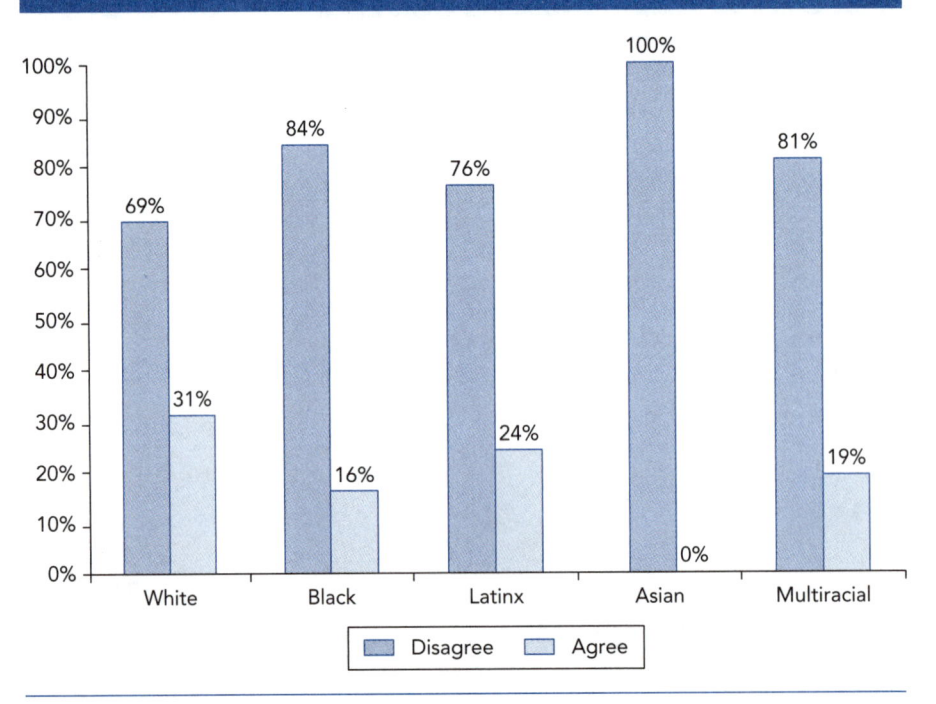

Race/Ethnicity	Disagree	Agree
White	69%	31%
Black	84%	16%
Latinx	76%	24%
Asian	100%	0%
Multiracial	81%	19%

conversation promotes the idea that "we need to have a standard." In reality, we actually need a cross-cultural standard.

Also prominent in deficit thinking is the presumption that individual behaviors and psychological dispositions are pervasive throughout a community. Figure 4.5 demonstrates whether teachers believe the values of disadvantaged communities go against school values. White educators are split—51% disagree, 49% agree. Black educators are less split—66% disagree, 34% agree. Latinx educators are similar—62% disagree, 38% agree. And multiracial educators maintain a similar pattern—65% disagree, 35% agree.

FIGURE 4.5 The percentage of educators by race/ethnicity who agree or disagree with the statement "The values and beliefs shared by those in disadvantaged neighborhoods tend to go against school values and beliefs about what makes up a good education"

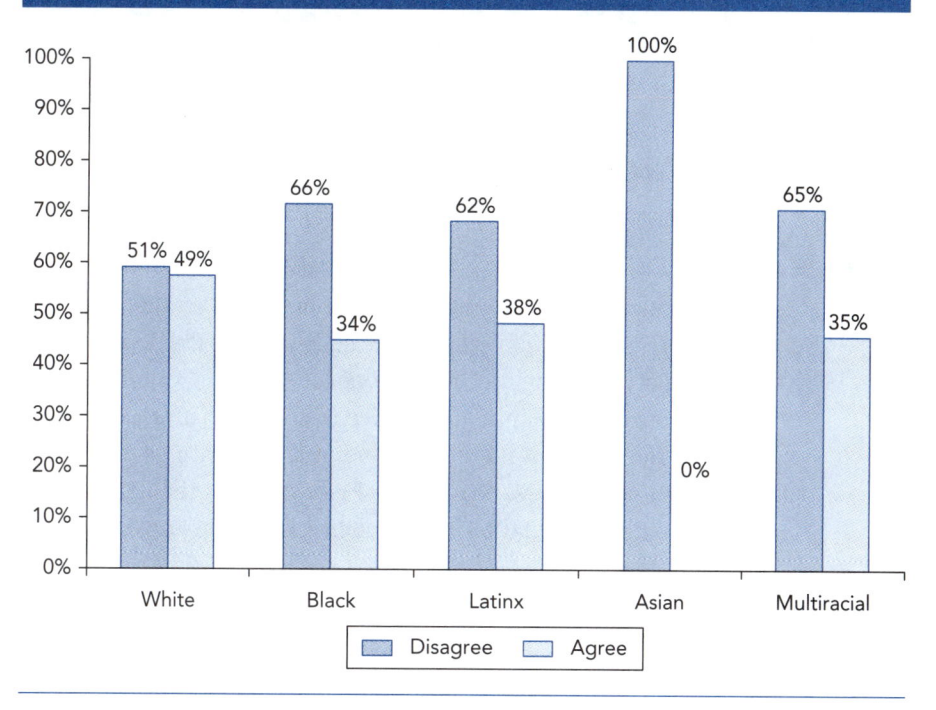

Race/Ethnicity	Disagree	Agree
White	51%	49%
Black	66%	34%
Latinx	62%	38%
Asian	100%	0%
Multiracial	65%	35%

Figure 4.6 shows educators as generally split on whether they consider an acculturation strategy as a means of addressing cultural deficit. In particular, a slight majority of White, Black, Latinx, and multiracial educators disagree that students of color should assimilate to succeed, while less than 50% agree. However, we also need to consider that each ethno-racial group maintains different definitions of assimilation as well as its relevance to succeeding in American culture.

FIGURE 4.6 The percentage of educators by race/ethnicity who agree or disagree with the statement "It is important that students of color assimilate so that they can succeed in mainstream American culture"

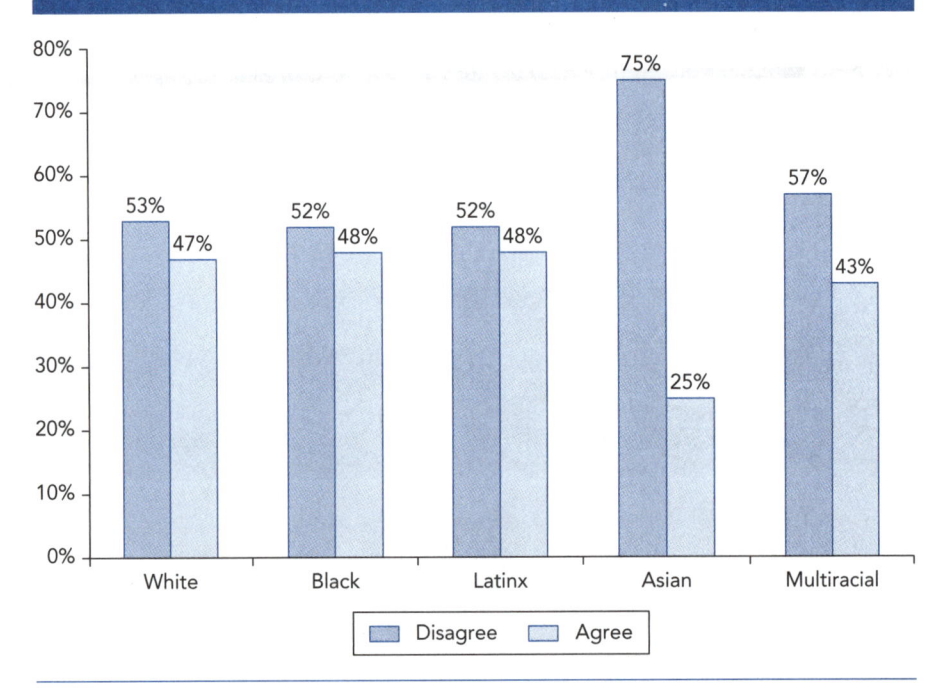

Race/Ethnicity	Disagree	Agree
White	53%	47%
Black	52%	48%
Latinx	52%	48%
Asian	75%	25%
Multiracial	57%	43%

As noted earlier, deficit thinking includes a presumption that individuals in low-income conditions experience such realities due to individual behaviors and psychological dispositions, such as not valuing education or demonstrating minimal initiative in school. Figure 4.7 demonstrates that more than 80% of educators disagree with such a belief. Unfortunately, slightly less than 20% of educators, at the highest end, maintain a deficit orientation that students from low-income homes show a lack of initiative.

Deficit thinking also includes the belief about genetic differences explaining achievement differences. Figure 4.8 indicates the percentage of educators who agree or disagree with sentiments about genetic differences. The majority of educators report not ascribing to this genetic pathology model. However, nearly 10% of those in each group ascribe to such a concept.

Deficit Thinking and Poverty Disciplining: Vignettes in Our Shopping Carts

The following vignettes are provided as an opportunity to practice understanding the dimensions of deficit thinking and poverty disciplining

FIGURE 4.7 The percentage of educators by race/ethnicity who agree or disagree with the statement "Students of color from disadvantaged homes just seem to show a lack of initiative"

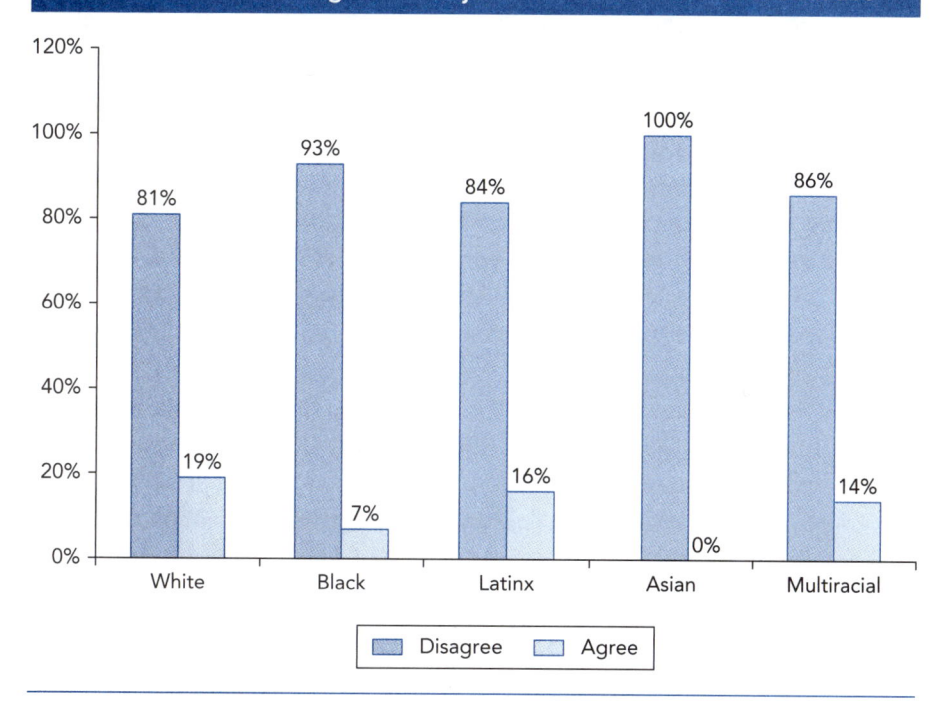

Race/Ethnicity	Disagree	Agree
White	81%	19%
Black	93%	7%
Latinx	84%	16%
Asian	100%	0%
Multiracial	86%	14%

FIGURE 4.8 The percentage of educators by race/ethnicity who agree or disagree with the statement "Although I am hesitant to say so publicly, I believe that racial differences in intelligence may have a hereditary or genetic component"

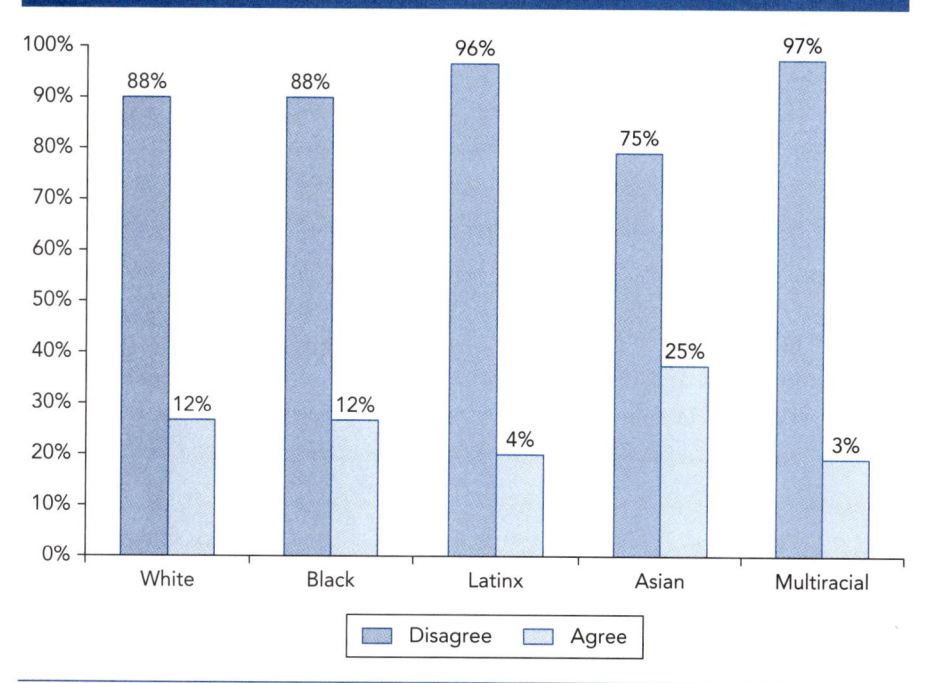

Race/Ethnicity	Disagree	Agree
White	88%	12%
Black	88%	12%
Latinx	96%	4%
Asian	75%	25%
Multiracial	97%	3%

occurring in our schools. In Appendix 3, I provide a tool for self-reflection on your lived experiences and their effect on your deficit thinking.

Vignette 1: They come from broken homes.

During a professional development session focused on reviewing data specific to disproportionate patterns of suspension, school district staff discussed the various theories—what I like to call their "professional hunches"—as to why these patterns exist. The Disproportionality Hunches exercise provides an opportunity for educators to discuss the various professional theories they've developed as a result of their experiences. More specifically, the worksheet allows for educators to brainstorm their various professional hunches and organize them using six quadrants: community, school, district, state, student, and classroom. Once complete with the brainstorm, these particular educators met in small groups to share their hunches. During the share-out, four educators shared a frustration. While a good portion of their hunches appeared in the school, classroom, and district quadrants, they did not like all the responsibility of the disproportionate patterns tying back to school and district practice. One educator stated, "How much farther do the standards need to be lowered for these students? They come from broken homes and just can't seem to learn how to do school. Why is it a problem to send them to special education services?"

Shopping Cart Experience: This response illustrates both genetic and cultural notions about individuals, in particular families living in low-income conditions. First, the framing of "lowering standards" operates from an associational bias allowing for a lowered cognitive capacity. At times, such a presumption originates from the idea of genetic or poverty-laden exposure instead of a consideration by this teacher that they lack the instructional skills to scaffold learning for a range of learners. Second, the framing of "broken homes" demonstrates an associational bias toward low-income homes as presumably "broken." And, lastly, this educator struggles with understanding how social institutions like schools are responsible for ensuring that associational biases do not prime the science of instruction and learning. Teachers may think: "I teach best when I get students who fit my affinity bias and comfort level." Educators play one of the most important roles in a student's learning. They will be more effective if they shun deficit orientations and instead embrace flexibility to respond to a variety of students' needs.

Vignette 2: The intervention system is built with a deficit frame.

During a root cause session with a district equity team, which consisted of the superintendent, other district leaders, principals, teachers, parents, and three students, we reviewed referral forms used across sample schools for recommending students to the tiered intervention system. In reviewing one school's form that included SGI (small-group instruction) as one of the pull-out intervention services, I turned to one of the students who attended the same school and asked, "Are you familiar with this process?" The student mentioned that he attended SGI. I then asked him to share with us about the process. I intended to understand whether the process on paper matches the experience of a student. The student described that he goes to a specific room during the SGI block, picks up a packet from the teacher's desk, and then sits alone to complete the packet. I asked the student whether the teacher comes around to help, and he replied no. He then proceeded to share that he goes there to complete those packets. As this district equity team listened, it became clear that the on-paper process did not fit the real-life enactment of SGI. In this way, research on the benefits of SGI were ignored. Even more poignant is how such intervention processes are conveyed as implemented well, and if students are not able to improve, then there must be something wrong with them.

Shopping Cart Experience: One outcome of a continuous diet of deficit orientations in "Title I schools" is a presumption that lower cognitive abilities exist among the student population. Research shows that in schools with a high proportion of students eligible for free or reduced-price lunch, teachers use instructional practices oriented toward remediation, or "skill and drill." These educators presume (1) students cannot progress if they don't know the basics; (2) students need repeated, and at times slower, exposure; and (3) students maintain slower learning rates and can't keep up with the pace of the curriculum. Overall, this type of systemic change to the true nature of SGI reduces learning to a solo activity of packet completion.

Vignette 3: The orphans need letters from our kids.

In 2019, during classroom observations of a suburban elementary school figuring out how to enact integration of Black and Latinx students with the White and Asian students on the other side of town, the principal and I walked into a classroom and saw a group of second graders writing letters. As we peeked in, we could see the students engrossed in their writing task and two additional adults (White women) observing. The teacher noticed us and came over to share that several parents were facilitating a community service activity with the students in which they would write encouraging letters to children who live in the orphanage in the urban city about 20 minutes away. The Black female principal and I both looked at each other, and asked about the orphanage. The teacher shared that the parents on the other side of town came up with the idea. "We thought it would be a good community service. Those orphans could use letters from our kids." The fact that the majority of the students in the room were White further complicated the experience because the students were performing a community action in which they could learn that orphans simply need emotional artifacts to help shift their condition. I approached some of the children to read their letters, and some included statements like "It'll get better," "I hope you can get a home like mine one day," and "I want to help you find a family like mine."

Shopping Cart Experience: In this example, the classroom participated in furthering a cultural notion that children in orphanages need messages from middle-class and affluent White children. The concern with this action involves the parents and educators operationalizing a White saviorism—the need to save the individual from their condition, with no regard for addressing the underlying systemic issue. The action of writing letters perpetuates a cultural notion of individualism. In other words, if individuals can just believe in themselves, their circumstances will change. This action prevents the opportunity to understand the systemic barriers playing a role in why children, particularly low-income and children of color, enter the foster care system.

Vignette 4: Why can't he understand that we are trying to help?

At the end of an equity session, a White male administrator approached me to share a personal concern for which he needed some advice. The administrator shared that his son, Jack, had a best friend, Jonathan, who is Black. The kids grew up together. During their senior year of high school, Jack shared with his dad that Jonathan decided not to apply to colleges because of the costs that his mother could not manage, in spite of his high regard as a soccer player. The administrator shared that he convinced Jonathan to apply to a variety of colleges in which he had contacts, one of which offered Jonathan a full athletic scholarship. The college was in the Midwest, however, and Jonathan lived in the Southeast. By the middle of summer, Jonathan had decided not to attend college and instead to work locally. The administrator felt hurt and shocked by Jonathan's decision and said, "Why can't he understand that we are trying to help? Why didn't he understand that this would change his circumstances?"

Shopping Cart Experience: In this example, the administrator struggled with understanding Jonathan's decision. However, the administrator was trapped in his own presumptions about economic conditions as individual and not systemic. In particular, attending college for individuals within families in low-income conditions means (1) providing financial support while in college, including the cost of books and weekend meals; (2) a missing income for the household; (3) ensuring the maintenance of academic progress and, in the instance of Jonathan, athletic progress; and (4) the unknown reality of being Black at a Predominantly White Institution (PWI) and enduring stereotype threats.

Vignette 5: Low-income students are in special education because of powerlines.

During a monthly check-in with an elementary school's equity team, one team member expressed confusion as to the root causes of the students' issues. The team member, and school psychologist, shared, "Why aren't we talking about the powerlines and the polluted river surrounding these kids?" I asked them to share more of their thinking. They proceeded to share that the low-income students, primarily overrepresented in special education, lived in a part of town with a lot of powerlines. "Don't you think that is impacting their cognitive ability?" Additionally, they shared that the students spent the summer swimming in a local river known to be polluted. I thanked them for sharing their perspective on environmental factors and encouraged them to consider (1) whether we have evidence of its impact on their students, and (2) the regulatory conditions that gave permission for the placement of such powerlines and the pollution of the river.

Shopping Cart Experience: In this example, the educator maintained a body of evidence in which environmental conditions seemed to have a biological impact on students, which translated into lowered cognitive abilities. Such conversations about environmental factors are pertinent. However, the concern is twofold: (1) How do such conversations situate the individuals impacted? Are they framed as making cultural or behavioral choices or affected by a systemic issue?—the solutions are oriented towards the frame—and (2) what relevance and influence do educators have about such environmental factors?—our concern should center on improving our instruction to be responsive.

Vignette 6: If Black people got health insurance, we wouldn't need to place their kids in special education.

During a monthly check-in with a middle school's equity team, one of the team members asked whether the issue of Black student overrepresentation in special education stems from a lack of health insurance. I asked them to expand on their thinking. The educator shared that they found Black people, particularly "low-income ones," lack health insurance and fail to seek health care. They suggested that the school should provide more information to Black families about getting health insurance. I thanked them for sharing their perspective and only responded to the policy suggestion of additional health insurance by reminding them of the Affordable Care Act.

Shopping Cart Experience: In this example, the educator maintains a set of understandings regarding the enrollment of students in special education as medically or biologically bound. In other words, the conditions with which students are diagnosed connect with some form of medical or biological need. Additionally, the educator has developed an associational bias about Black people that includes a presumption of limited health insurance and the need for more insurance.

Vignette 7: We took away the toilet paper . . . because they act like animals.

During a yearlong school reform project, I focused on supporting the instructional turnaround work of a high school, which involved conducting walk-throughs of classrooms with the principal using an observation tool. In between two classroom visits, I needed to use the restroom and asked for the location of the nearest one. As I entered the restroom, I immediately noticed the stalls did not have doors and, on closer examination, that each stall was missing toilet paper. Upon leaving the restroom, I asked the principal why the stalls were missing doors and toilet paper. He remarked that the students behaved like animals and stuffed the toilets with paper, so the school removed the doors and the paper. I asked what happens when female students go to the restroom. He stated that they are required to ask for toilet paper from the teacher. The school rations the paper so they do not overflow the toilets.

Shopping Cart Experience: A common association is made between poverty status and "culture of poverty" as demonstrative of behaviors counter to the discipline code. The bias of this perspective lies in its assumptions that all individuals living in low-income conditions behave similarly. Several difficulties characterize this biased viewpoint: (1) the presumption that responding to students in this manner is developmentally appropriate; (2) a bias toward female students layered in the response; and (3) the idea that disciplining children from poor conditions will minimize "poverty behavior" and enhance academic engagement.

Vignette 8: Can you talk to my Black kids so they can hear an articulate Black person?

During a school visit, I conducted a walk-through with a high school principal and observed different classrooms. One was a U.S. government class, composed of about 30 students, about half Black. The teacher, a White male, was reviewing the Supreme Court history. As I stepped out with the principal, the social studies teacher asked for my opinion, and I shared some generic thoughts about the content and my own experience teaching the subject. The teacher then remarked that he found me very articulate and wondered if I would come back and talk to his Black students "so they can hear an articulate Black person."

Shopping Cart Experience: Low-income status and racial groups have a linguistic association. The bias viewpoint shared in this vignette (1) assumes the linguistic capacity of Black students as inarticulate or noncommunicative; (2) presumes my diction and display exemplifies the Blackness that the students need to demonstrate; and (3) presumes that Black students simply changing their linguistic style will improve their social and academic outcomes.

The work raised in this chapter is daunting. Remember that we have a lifetime of experiences in our shopping carts that require unpacking. We are all well-intentioned individuals with a long history of oppressive ideas baked into how our society operates. This chapter encourages us to take the time to reflect on how these deficit thinking and poverty disciplining ideologies show up for us. The following questions point to specific areas for reflection. Additionally, Appendix 5 provides a tool for further reflection on the vignettes. In the next chapter, I provide a road map of the replacement ideologies, mindsets, and beliefs we need for supporting a more just and equitable school system.

Chapter Reflection Questions

These reflection questions are intended to encourage unpacking and replacing of our shopping carts.

1. What were your thoughts on deficit thinking and poverty disciplining ideologies before reading this chapter? Have your ideas changed?

2. How do you experience poverty in your day-to-day lived experience? How do you process those experiences?

3. How do you experience patterns of poverty inequality in your day-to-day lived experience? How do you process those experiences?

4. Did a particular vignette stand out for you? Why?

Interrupting Bias-Based Beliefs Built on Whiteness

5

> If a person is capable of rectifying his erroneous judgments in the light of new evidence he is not prejudiced. Prejudgments become prejudices only if they are not reversible when exposed to new knowledge. A prejudice, unlike a simple misconception, is actively resistant to all evidence that would unseat it. We tend to grow emotional when a prejudice is threatened with contradiction. Thus the difference between ordinary prejudgments and prejudice is that one can discuss and rectify a prejudgment without emotional resistance. (Allport, 1968, p. 9)

These prejudgments have a continuous presence in our shopping carts. Gordon Allport's (1968) reference to prejudgments allows us to understand that exposure to a continuous diet of Whiteness-framed affinity and associational bias fuels those prejudgments. Such ongoing affinity and associational bias exposure leads to a range of prejudgments about groups that get translated into practices, processes, policies, and individual behaviors. For example, when my oldest child attended elementary school during the 2000s, one of their teachers, a White woman, taught a lesson on Black history. In the middle of class, she said to my child, "Javier, I'm sure your parents' family has talked about the civil rights movement and what they did during that time." My child, ever his usual quick-witted self, replied, "My dad is Panamanian and wasn't born here, and my mom is Puerto Rican." Taken aback, the teacher in that moment realized how she relied on my child's Brown skin color as a singular marker of an African American identification—showcasing a limitation of cultural knowledge due to continuous affinity bias and a simplified association of skin color with specific ethno-racial identities.

Such moments seem relatively harmless compared to others that demonstrate a level of hostility, which I consider demonstrative of prejudice. For instance, in high school my oldest child walked into science class wearing a hoodie, and the White male science teacher proceeded to tell my child, "Take off your hoodie. That's why you people get shot." In that moment, the prejudgment carried a disdain toward "you people" that implied the potential of moving from prejudgment to prejudice for this teacher. Whiteness justified and set the stage for this teacher's prejudgment and prejudice toward Black and Brown bodies as appropriately invoking fear and violence imposed upon them.

To contend with these various forms of Whiteness-derived prejudgments as they appear in practice, processes, procedures, and policies, I draw on Gordon Allport's (1968) work on contact theory, viewed as the hallmark of social psychology research and theory regarding prejudice and its interruption. Key for us to understand in education is that, as educators, we need to accept that we and our colleagues carry prejudgments through affinity and associational biases that manifest in colorblindness, deficit thinking, and poverty disciplining beliefs. Though prejudice likely presents as well among staff in school, prejudice is difficult to overcome and beyond the scope and intention of this chapter. Instead, I focus herein on the ways in which as individual educators we can choose to interrupt the nature of Whiteness-derived prejudgments existing in our shopping carts and their related beliefs, colorblindness, deficit thinking, and poverty disciplining, which we weaponize in school practices to devalue minoritized populations.

This chapter emphasizes replacing those bias-based beliefs as a way to interrupt the hold of Whiteness ideology in schools. I draw on social psychology contact theories to provide an operating framework for school practitioners to construct experiences that reframe race, ethnicity, language, gender expression, and sexuality diversity as assets. In addition, the chapter underscores use of an asset-based notion of diversity (cross-cultural skills) as a foundation for developing replacement beliefs and related behaviors, and is organized into two subsections:

1. Foundational content on contact theory and cross-cultural skills and dispositions

2. Foundational strategies for practicing cross-cultural skills to interrupt affinity and associational bias frames of colorblindness, deficit thinking, and poverty disciplining beliefs, including examples of activities for how to interrupt and replace the Whiteness-derived prejudgments and beliefs

Contact Theory, Cross-Cultural Skills, and How They Help Fix Our Shopping Carts

Gordon Allport's (1968) original research on contact theory and the follow-up research from many social psychologists (Pettigrew, 1998, 2006) continue to frame the idea of contact theory and the ways to interrupt our biases. Contact theory hypothesizes that continuous contact between different groups can reduce prejudice—an idea that many of us carry for solving the issues of discrimination and inequality. For example, in 2021, I supported a school district cited for disproportionality in suspension. During a meeting with the superintendent and the assistant superintendent, both White identifying, they shared that the local school board elections were taking a different approach. One of the school board candidates was passing around flyers, with a picture of me, stating, "We will get the King of Critical Race Theory out of our schools." In this current moment, such antics are not surprising. The superintendent then shared, "I don't understand why they are resisting this. If they would just get to know you, they would understand." From his vantage point, mere contact and engagement would solve this issue. However, much more has to occur for contact to take root.

Allport's (1954) original research on prejudice noted four dynamics that allowed for interruption of prejudgment and prejudice: (1) equal group status in the intergroup experience; (2) common goals desired in the intergroup experience; (3) intergroup cooperation; and (4) support of authority. Let's discuss these four dynamics, referred to as facilitation elements rather than essential conditions for intergroup contact (Pettigrew, 1998).

1. *Equal group status:* In this condition, individuals *enter* intergroup experiences with equal status. For instance, if teachers of various demographics enter a meeting or gathering in which intergroup contact occurs, they must enter with equal status in their role, responsibility, and commitment to supporting students. Similarly, if parents attend an international food dinner, a children's play, or a sporting event held at a school, they enter as equal parents who care for their children. The equal status allows for the recognition in schools that individuals maintain a similar status and value as a teacher or parent. This requires understanding racial, ethnic, language, gender, and sexuality differences as valuable and having equal cultural status.

2. *Common Goals:* Under this condition, the intergroup experience can be facilitated when group members seek a common goal. When

a sports team seeks to defeat an opposing team, for example, the team members share a common goal. Among teachers, this might mean working on the solution to a problem that has beneficial importance for each individual, such as lunch duties, school drop-off or pickup, or the best time for school announcements. Pursuing a common goal facilitates consideration of each individual's contribution and lessens a continuous attention to a stereotype. In other words, conversations centered on the common goal reduce the habit of thinking about stereotypes of marginalized populations. For instance, at a middle school seventh-grade team meeting, a Black male teacher raised a concern about how two students, one Black and one Asian, had fought and how the Black student received a four-day out-of-school suspension while the Asian student got in-school suspension. The Black male teacher's White colleagues reasoned, "That student was more aggressive during the fight," and "That student has a history." In that moment, these teachers did not share a common goal of addressing racial differences in discipline consequences. Additionally, the group did not maintain enough equity literacy even to consider addressing racial differences as a common or shared goal. In this instance, the Black male educator may have achieved more traction by framing an audit-type conversation about discipline practices and consequences. The conversation might have gone differently if he had asked, "How have we engaged in discipline practices over the last month?"

3. *Intergroup Cooperation:* In this condition, the intergroup experience must involve a cooperative environment, not a competition. This collaborative experience in an intergroup dynamic allows for overriding stereotypes within the context of group work. Members will eventually develop an understanding of each other as critical contributors. For example, when teachers are working in a Professional Learning Community (PLC) setting or grade-level environment, they must center on collaborative talk: "How do we all solve this problem?" or "What is the best way for our unit to implement this?" and "I value the different perspectives each team member offers."

4. *Support of Authority:* In this condition, the intergroup experience necessitates validation from an authoritative figure. In schools, this involves leadership stating explicitly that integration in curricular and social interaction is necessary to address disproportionate patterns, to develop a strong pedagogical environment, to improve tiered interventions, and so on. School or district leadership must

continuously reinforce this message and provide the resources to support it, which may involve an equity director with responsibility and authority; school-level equity goals that focus on curricular, practice, and process changes (not simply book clubs); school board meetings that discuss initiatives to address disparity goals; and district leadership, especially superintendents, who embody cross-cultural skills as demonstrated through continuous engagements with marginalized communities.

> ### Shopping Cart Exploration Pause
>
> 1. Do you recognize these conditions in your school? Home?
>
> 2. What conditions do you find difficult to develop? What conditions do you find manageable to develop?
>
> 3. What may be some social or cultural impediments and strengths in your environments that can support development of these conditions?

These conditions are important in schools in order for educators to address patterns of racial/ethnic, linguistic, and gender disparity and to manage the ways in which Whiteness ideology may experience a sense of social threat regarding resources and identity. In other words, Whiteness ideology has constructed a normalization that primes school resources, curriculum, instruction, and staffing to largely serve middle-class, heterosexual, two-parent, English-speaking, and/or White-identifying communities. Under the four conditions, (1) shared cross-culturally based common goals allow for Whiteness ideology to understand that such goals benefit students' humanity; (2) equal status allows for Whiteness to understand that "within equal status" means dissipating ideas of "one right way" and allowing for multiple statuses to have equal standard; (3) intergroup cooperation allows for Whiteness ideology to practice experiencing White identity primacy as a sheltered existence; and (4) support from authority allows for Whiteness ideology to recognize authorities and authorization as central in this journey and as reinforcing cross-cultural skills. Setting these conditions is important. However, what skills do educators need to embody while engaging in these integrated contact experiences? We must consider next the cross-cultural skills that we need to practice in order to diminish the presence of Whiteness ideology.

Cross-Cultural Skills The concept of cross-cultural knowledge and skills emerged in the late 1970s to explain the components of cross-cultural competence. We now understand its two major elements: (1) the psychological and emotional well-being of a person, and (2) the person's ability to fit in or negotiate new environments (Chiu et al., 2013). In other words, we can think of cross-cultural competence as a "set of attitudes, knowledge and skills that together form a personal attribute that facilitates smooth and effective communication and interaction with people who are culturally and linguistically different" (Lonner, 2014, p. 856; see also J. Wilson et al., 2013).

Let's start with the first component of cross-cultural knowledge and skills: *psychological and emotional well-being.* In other words, each person must reflect on their cultural empathy, open-mindedness, social initiative, emotional stability, and flexibility when interacting with different people (van der Zee & van Oudenhoven, 2000). Such skills appear in the ability to listen to and experience cultures that differ from our own with a disposition of "This is a new experience of learning." In particular, we must not assess the new experience as less than or of an inferior status than our own cultural custom. For instance, when visiting another country and learning that driving occurs on the opposite side of the road than we may be accustomed to, we must have cultural empathy for this new experience of driving versus having the view of cultural diminishment in which we think, "Why do they drive on the wrong side of the street?" The trait of cultural diminishment is of significance because Whiteness ideology utilizes colorblindness, deficit thinking, and poverty disciplining mindsets to enact diminishment.

For example, in 2016, I worked with a district marked by racially and economically segregated schools. During one of my visits to an elementary school in an affluent part of the city, the few Black kids who attended the school arrived by bus while hundreds of White children walked to school with their parents. Interestingly, all the White children arrived at the playground, located at the back of the school, to run around. Meanwhile, the school bus delivered the Black children to the front of the school, where they were escorted to the cafeteria. The principal rationalized the difference as needing to provide the "bus kids" with breakfast. In that instance, the principal lacked the cultural empathy and flexibility to understand the Black children's need to be seen as needing time to enjoy the playground, not to be simplified as "in need." The capacity to develop cultural empathy, flexibility, and cultural sensitivity requires a simultaneous reduction of a colorblindness ideology. That is, you cannot have cultural empathy for a group while viewing their racial identity as nonexistent or irrelevant. Ignoring race gives permission for the denial of humanity toward Black, Brown, and Indigenous populations. Thus, the psychological and emotional well-being of a person, including cultural empathy, open-mindedness, and social initiative, requires interruption of colorblindness, deficit thinking, and poverty disciplining beliefs.

We can think of the second component of cross-cultural competence as the skills necessary to be cross-cultural: *the ability to fit into new environments.* In other words, the ways we talk, behave, and interact in social situations such as school can enhance the comfort and malleability of development. Some examples of cross-cultural skills include reflecting and seeking feedback on intercultural encounters, developing reliable information sources on cultures, learning about cultures, engaging in disciplined self-presentation (i.e., paying attention to how one's cultural presentations are layered with Whiteness), coping with cultural surprises, taking perspectives of others, and understanding oneself in cultural contexts (Rasmussen & Sieck, 2015). These types of skills are valuable for developing cross-cultural competency. However, it cannot be overemphasized how this competency requires a nurturing environment. In other words, we need to understand how to develop these skills when we may live in a segregated neighborhood, work in a segregated school environment, remain surrounded by other individuals not keen on developing cross-cultural skills, or work for district or school leadership sporadic in prioritizing diversity, equity, and inclusion.

Rasmussen and Sieck (2015) outlined a range of cross-cultural competencies that we can understand as skills and attitudes developed from intergroup experiences. Let's talk through these skills and attitudes in our everyday lived experiences.

- *Diplomatic Mindset:* This domain refers to a person's understanding that intercultural interactions or relationships can have a personal and/or work-related benefit. For instance, the diplomatic mindset of a teacher approaching an intercultural interaction with parents of students who speak a different language would involve them learning phrases from the parents' language. The teacher gains cultural insight as well as social capital by investing in the expansion of their own cross-cultural tool kit.

- *Cultural Reasoning:* This domain refers to a person's ability to make sense of culturally different experiences such as encountering how various groups celebrate different holidays, drive on different sides of the road, and dress in different styles. In school settings, cultural reasoning is an important skill for understanding student misbehaviors, interacting with parents who speak a language other than English, visiting the home of a student, and so on. To put the skill in practice, we need to reach a level of perspective-taking that allows us to develop the cross-cultural ability to understand something from a different cultural seat than our own.

- *Intercultural Interaction:* This domain refers to a person's ability to communicate and interact with individuals who identify differently than themselves through a disciplined manner. That is, if you walk into a mosque, you follow the cultural customs of removing your shoes. If you enter a Catholic church during mass, you follow the custom of silence. This skill requires at least a cursory level of cultural knowledge not steeped in stereotype to guide the intercultural interaction.

- *Cultural Learning:* This domain refers to a person's ability to gather new cultural knowledge and put it to use within social interactions and work-related tasks. The gathering process involves relying on credible sources and maintaining an understanding of self within that exploration. That means, if interested in learning about cowboy culture, preparing yourself to visit a cowboy ranch to learn about their cultural customs and ask questions steeped in curiosity rather than stereotype. Instead of asking "Is it true that . . . ," say, "I'm interested in learning more about . . ." In schools, cultural learning skills among educators involve understanding that adding a new volume of "culturally diverse" books requires the educator to maintain cultural knowledge regarding the topic or theme. For example, reading *The Hate U Give* (Thomas, 2017) requires cultural knowledge about policing and its history within Black communities.

These skills and competencies are important to explore in our personal lives, and Appendix 4 provides a tool to help you consider how these skills currently exist and are absent in your life. In the following section, I discuss the types of experiences necessary to fill our shopping carts to develop the knowledge, feelings, and skills to be cross-cultural, even within environments not supportive of such pedagogical and personal development.

Shopping Cart Exploration Pause

1. What skills do you find yourself most comfortable practicing?
2. What skills do you find yourself needing support to practice?
3. What skills resonate the most for you? Why?

Strategies for Cross-Cultural Development and Bias-Based Belief Interruption

Educators can practice the following three strategies for developing cross-cultural competencies in their shopping carts.

Strategy 1—Counter-Stereotypic Imaging: Stereotypes abound throughout society. However, entrenched within the psyche, they can operate as automatic mental schemas (Bodenhausen et al., 2009). Counter-stereotypic imaging is used to challenge the truthfulness of a stereotype (Blair et al., 2001). This strategy involves oversaturating the environment with counter-stereotypes to reduce the relevance of such stereotypes. As demonstrated in Figure 5.1, this might include books used in classrooms, images portrayed in the classroom and hallways, students used in leadership roles, the participation of students in advanced courses, and so on.

FIGURE 5.1 List of Activities (Counter-Stereotypic Imaging)

Activities	Cross-cultural skills:	School-level activity	Individual-level activity
	• Diplomatic mindset • Cultural reasoning • Intercultural interaction • Cultural learning		
Diversify books in classrooms and libraries with a focus on identity representation and diverse narratives of identities (savior, supporter, superhero, etc.)	• Cultural reasoning • Cultural learning	X	
Engage in curricular and lesson planning that utilizes historically responsive literacy (Muhammad, 2017) for transforming the colorblind curriculum and lesson plan frameworks	• Cultural reasoning • Cultural learning	X	
Attend cultural community events such as library fairs, street fairs, heritage month school and community events, annual parades (Chinese New Year, St. Patrick's Day, Pride Month, etc.), and so on	• Cultural reasoning • Intercultural interaction • Cultural learning		X

Strategy 2—Intergroup Contact and Individuating: As early as the 1960s, scholars discussed intergroup contact as a strategy for reducing/interrupting the reliance on implicit biases and bias-based beliefs. The interaction focuses on sharing cultural artifacts within a context of parity and equal standing (Pettigrew, 1998; Pettigrew & Tropp, 2006). The intergroup contact allows for individuating, or seeing each experience as

specific to an individual and not a group, which minimizes adherence to and challenges stereotypes. Stereotypes are at times derived from imagery of outgroup members and used to maintain ingroup status as well. To counteract these stereotypes, individuating is a proven strategy for creating information specific to individuals that allows for less reliance on a stereotype (Fiske, 1998). Individuating involves ongoing, positive, equal sharing of information and sustained interaction. This strategy must occur within authentic and deliberate experiences, as shown in Figure 5.2, such as attending grocery stores in a different neighborhood and attending functions such as art exhibits that showcase cultural groups less familiar.

FIGURE 5.2 List of Activities (Intergroup Contact and Individuating)

Activities	Cross-cultural skills: • Diplomatic mindset • Cultural reasoning • Intercultural interaction • Cultural learning	School-level activity	Individual-level activity
Arrange monthly/bimonthly school events for parents that involve activities to encourage interaction between parents	• Cultural reasoning • Intercultural interaction • Cultural learning	X	
Attend school sports events that encourage collaborative talk and support (e.g., create sections in bleachers and provide spectators a cheer to practice before showcasing during sporting event)	• Cultural reasoning • Intercultural interaction • Cultural learning	X	
Start a club among school staff to encourage meeting a new person every two months, and provide incentives for the get-together	• Cultural reasoning • Intercultural interaction • Cultural learning	X	
If you participate in a sport, visit parks in different parts of your town that reflect other groups (e.g., join running groups with an explicit intention to recruit a diversity of participants)	• Cultural reasoning • Intercultural interaction • Cultural learning		X
If interested in developing language skills other than your own, immerse yourself in everyday activities (grocery shopping, eating at a restaurant, using a car wash, etc.) in a neighborhood where that language is primary.	• Cultural reasoning • Intercultural interaction • Cultural learning		X

Strategy 3—Perspective-Taking: This strategy focuses on creating opportunities for an individual to develop a closeness with a stigmatized and marginalized group and reduce the habit of using stereotypes (Galinsky & Moskowitz, 2000). Perspective-taking involves development of cultural learning schemas through sustained individuating interactions or other means of experiences, which engages the individual in experiencing a condition different from their own. In this way, they have an opportunity to develop an understanding of the cultural schemas that emerge as a result of that specific condition. For example, individuals may live on food stamps or cash assistance for a week to understand how individuals living in such a condition make reasoned decisions. Teachers may walk the routes that students take to get back and forth to school or periodically sit at lunchroom tables of stigmatized and marginalized groups to listen to their stories of school. See Figure 5.3 for additional examples.

FIGURE 5.3   List of Activities (Perspective-Taking)

Activities	Cross-cultural skills: <ul><li>Diplomatic mindset</li><li>Cultural reasoning</li><li>Intercultural interaction</li><li>Cultural learning</li></ul>	School-level activity	Individual-level activity
Shadow various students who represent groups experiencing marginalization (e.g., multilanguage learners, students receiving numerous behavioral referrals or suspensions, racial/ethnic minoritized groups)	<ul><li>Cultural reasoning</li><li>Intercultural interaction</li><li>Cultural learning</li></ul>	X	
Attend school ethnic pride events of groups that you are less familiar with and desire to engage more earnestly	<ul><li>Cultural reasoning</li><li>Intercultural interaction</li><li>Cultural learning</li></ul>	X	
Start a club among school staff to encourage meeting a new person every two months, and provide incentives for the get-together	<ul><li>Cultural reasoning</li><li>Intercultural interaction</li><li>Cultural learning</li></ul>	X	
Join a book club at a local bookstore in which a diversity of authors do book readings or a diversity of books are discussed	<ul><li>Cultural reasoning</li><li>Intercultural interaction</li><li>Cultural learning</li></ul>		X
Read stories about people from other countries, talk about how their daily lives differ from your own, and discuss how their environment has impacted their day-to-day lives	<ul><li>Cultural reasoning</li><li>Intercultural interaction</li><li>Cultural learning</li></ul>	X	X

In Appendix 6, I provide additional tools to support your exploration, as well as tools that you can use to collaborate with other educators and perhaps conduct some of this work as an entire school community. As I outlined in the Introduction, as educators we are charged with interrupting the original sin of Whiteness that continues to operate in our school processes. Our greatest tool is the will and desire to be cross-cultural human beings not only to heal our oppressive traumas, but also to develop schools that provide cross-culturally healing and supporting spaces for children.

Overall, this book intends to provide you with a personal journey to take as part of the charge that Black, Mexican, Native American, and Asian families led by suing the local government and requesting humanity, integration, and equality. We have not had an opportunity to explicitly discuss the fundamental role of Whiteness ideology in the social fabric of where we live, who we go to school with, who we work with, and where we shop and eat. As I stated at the beginning of this book, such discussion provides us with a way to understand historically how this ideology has been baked into our psyche, but also that it can be remedied. With intentional attention to how this ideology exists and the desire to dismantle—and replace—it, we can support the quest given to us by *Brown v. Board*.

Appendices

Appendix 1: Reflecting on Our Whiteness Exposure

Appendix 2: Shopping Cart List of Experiences: Everyday Colorblindness and Color Evasiveness

Appendix 3: Colorblindness Reflection Activity

Appendix 4: Shopping Cart List of Experiences: Everyday Deficit Thinking and Poverty Disciplining

Appendix 5: Deficit Thinking and Poverty Disciplining Reflection Activity

Appendix 6: Exploring Our Current Cross-Cultural Lives, Skills, and Competencies

Appendix 7: Additional Cross-Cultural Activities

Appendix 8: Professional Development Template for Equity Belief Work: School Equity Team Tool

Appendix 1
Reflecting on Our Whiteness Exposure

Whiteness operates with a sentiment of centrality: *White identity as normed and standard.* Such exposure can create gaps in cultural knowledge and eventually skills necessary for social interaction. The following tool is intended to be used as a group exercise.

Instructions: Complete the worksheet as an individual. You should anticipate having empty boxes in the grid. After completing the worksheet alone, gather with two or three additional individuals and share what you know, who or what taught you, and what you need to learn. The intention of these ongoing conversations is to center the concepts that Whiteness distracts us from learning.

APPENDIX 1. REFLECTING ON OUR WHITENESS EXPOSURE

		KNOW *WHAT DO YOU KNOW ABOUT THE TOPIC?*	**WHO OR WHAT** *WHO OR WHAT TAUGHT YOU ABOUT THE TOPIC?*	**NEED TO LEARN** *WHAT DO YOU NEED TO LEARN?*
Race	• Racial groups • Racial identification			
Ethnicity	• Ethnic groups • Ethnic identification			
Sexuality	• Sexuality groups • Sexuality identification			
Language	• Language identification			
Income	• Income groups • Income status identification			

Appendix 2
Shopping Cart List of Experiences

Everyday Colorblindness and Color Evasiveness

Instructions: Complete the worksheet as an individual. You should anticipate having empty boxes in the grid. After completing the worksheet alone, gather with two or three additional individuals and share how these experiences gave you language about identities.

LIST OF EXPERIENCES	WHAT DID THIS EXPERIENCE PROVIDE IN UNDERSTANDING RACE, ETHNICITY, LANGUAGE, GENDER, OR SEXUALITY DIFFERENCE?	WHAT'S BEEN YOUR CROSS-CULTURAL EXPERIENCE OR EXPANSION IN BEING WITH DIFFERENT RACIAL, ETHNIC, LANGUAGE, GENDER, AND SEXUALITY GROUPS?
Neighborhoods you lived in before the age of 18		
Neighborhoods you lived in after age 18		
Close friends		
Events you attend for celebratory months (Black History, Hispanic Heritage, Native American Heritage, Pride, etc.)		
Supermarkets/grocery stores		
Shopping malls		
College friendships		
Faith-based places		

Appendix 3
Colorblindness Reflection Activity

The following reflection activity is intended to provide educators an opportunity to practice understanding colorblindness. This practice involves being able to identify the types of social identities made invisible in each vignette and brainstorm ways in which to address the issue in the moment or over time. At times, the difficulty with addressing bias-based beliefs involves not knowing what to say. This reflection activity is intended to give practice in this regard.

APPENDIX 3. COLORBLINDNESS REFLECTION ACTIVITY

	WHAT IDENTITIES WERE MADE SOCIALLY ABSENT IN THIS EXAMPLE?	BRAINSTORM STRATEGIES FOR ADDRESSING THIS SITUATION
Vignette 1		
Vignette 2		
Vignette 3		
Vignette 4		
Vignette 5		
Vignette 6		
Vignette 7		
Vignette 8		
Vignette 9		
Vignette 10		

Appendix 4
Shopping Cart List of Experiences

Everyday Deficit Thinking and Poverty Disciplining

Instructions: Complete the worksheet as an individual. You should anticipate having empty boxes in the grid. After completing the worksheet alone, gather with two or three additional individuals and share how these experiences gave you language about identities. The intention of these ongoing conversations is to center the concepts that Whiteness distracts us from learning.

APPENDIX 4. SHOPPING CART LIST OF EXPERIENCES

LIST OF EXPERIENCES	WHAT DID THIS EXPERIENCE PROVIDE IN UNDERSTANDING SOCIOECONOMIC STATUS DIFFERENCES?	WHAT'S BEEN YOUR CROSS-CULTURAL EXPERIENCE OR EXPANSION IN BEING WITH DIFFERENT SOCIOECONOMIC GROUPS?
Neighborhoods you lived in before the age of 18		
Neighborhoods you lived in after age 18		
Close friends		
Supermarkets/grocery stores		
Shopping malls		
College friendships		
Faith-based places		

Appendix 5
Deficit Thinking and Poverty Disciplining Reflection Activity

The following reflection activity is intended to provide leaders an opportunity to practice understanding deficit thinking and poverty disciplining. This practice involves being able to identify the types of social identities framed as deficient in each vignette and brainstorm ways in which to address the issue in the moment or over time. At times, the difficulty with addressing bias-based beliefs involves not knowing what to say. This reflection activity is intended to give practice in this regard.

APPENDIX 5. DEFICIT THINKING AND POVERTY DISCIPLINING REFLECTION ACTIVITY

	WHAT IDENTITIES WERE MADE SOCIALLY DEFICIENT IN THIS EXAMPLE?	BRAINSTORM STRATEGIES FOR ADDRESSING THIS SITUATION
Vignette 1		
Vignette 2		
Vignette 3		
Vignette 4		
Vignette 5		
Vignette 6		
Vignette 7		
Vignette 8		

Appendix 6
Exploring Our Current Cross-Cultural Lives, Skills, and Competencies

Instructions: Complete the worksheet as an individual. The self-assessment column involves asking yourself the question "How do I [insert one of the definitions]?" For example, "How do I maintain a mission orientation about culture?" You should anticipate having empty boxes in the grid. After completing the worksheet alone, gather with two or three additional individuals and share your self-assessment. The intention of these ongoing conversations is to center the concepts that Whiteness distracts us from learning. After completing the activity, discuss your self-assessment with others and consider the following next steps: (1) notice your strengths and areas of improvement; (2) consider how your environments support and detract from your cross-cultural development; and (3) identify one or two competencies to practice over a six- to twelve-month period.

	DEFINITION	**SELF-ASSESSMENT HOW DO I . . .**
Diplomatic Mindset	• Maintains a mission orientation about culture • Manages attitudes toward culture • Understands self in cultural context	
Cultural Reasoning	• Copes with cultural surprises • Takes perspective of others in intercultural interactions • Develops cultural explanations of behavior	
Intercultural Interaction	• Engages in disciplined self-presentation • Plans intercultural communications • Acts with limited cultural knowledge	
Cultural Learning	• Is self-directed in learning about cultures • Develops reliable information sources • Reflects and seeks feedback on intercultural encounters	

Source: Rasmussen and Sieck (2015).

Appendix 7
Additional Cross-Cultural Activities

The following list is reflective of the activities found in Chapter 5 of *Solving Disproportionality and Achieving Equity* (Fergus, 2016a). The list also contains the interruption strategy that is primary in the activity.

ACTIVITY	PURPOSE	PROMINENT INTERRUPTION STRATEGY
ACTIVITY 1.1: *Build a common definition of educational equity.*	Practitioners learn definitions of educational equity. This activity provides an opportunity for biased views (i.e., deficit thinking, colorblindness, and poverty disciplining) to emerge, to be discussed, and to potentially be replaced.	Perspective-Taking
ACTIVITY 1.2: *Practice applying definitions of educational equity.*	Practitioners apply new definitions of educational equity. This activity provides an opportunity for biased views (i.e., deficit thinking, colorblindness, and poverty disciplining) to emerge, to be discussed, and to potentially be replaced.	Perspective-Taking
ACTIVITY 1.3: *Creating Schoolwide Equity Principles*	Practitioners define schoolwide principles of educational equity. This activity is intended for significant group discussion that leads to the highlighting of five core principles.	Perspective-Taking Individuation Intergroup Contact (Note: dependent on racial and ethnic diversity of staff)

APPENDIX 7. ADDITIONAL CROSS-CULTURAL ACTIVITIES   141

ACTIVITY	PURPOSE	PROMINENT INTERRUPTION STRATEGY
ACTIVITY 2.1.1: *Unpacking the Deficit Thinking Elephant*	Provide practitioners an opportunity to consider how deficit thinking as an ideology relies on consistently framing the abilities and behaviors of low-income and racial/ethnic minority students with a deficit orientation.	Perspective-Taking Individuation
ACTIVITY 2.1.2: *Unpacking the Deficit Thinking Elephant—Survey Activity*	Using a survey activity, provide practitioners an opportunity to consider how deficit thinking as an ideology relies on consistently framing the abilities and behaviors of low-income and racial/ethnic minority students with a deficit orientation.	Perspective-Taking Individuation
ACTIVITY 2.2: *Replacing the Deficit Thinking Elephant*	Provide practitioners an opportunity to *replace* deficit thinking ideology that relies on consistently framing the abilities and behaviors of low-income and racial/ethnic minority students with a deficit orientation.	Perspective-Taking Individuation Improved Decision-Making
ACTIVITY 2.3.1: *Unpacking the Poverty Disciplining Elephant*	Provide practitioners an opportunity to consider how poverty disciplining as an ideology relies on consistently framing the abilities and behaviors of low-income and racial/ethnic minority students with a deficit orientation, and give them "universal" behaviors for success.	Perspective-Taking Individuation
ACTIVITY 2.3.2: *Unpacking the Poverty Disciplining Elephant*	Using a survey activity, provide practitioners an opportunity to consider how poverty disciplining as an ideology relies on consistently framing the abilities and behaviors of low-income and racial/ethnic minority students with a deficit orientation, and give them "universal" behaviors for success.	Perspective-Taking Individuation
ACTIVITY 2.4: *Meritocracy Line*	Have practitioners consider that class-based structures have the effect of advancing some individuals and holding others back.	Perspective-Taking Individuation Intergroup Contact

(Continued)

(Continued)

ACTIVITY	PURPOSE	PROMINENT INTERRUPTION STRATEGY
ACTIVITY 2.5: *Schools Are Protective, Not Risky Environments*	Have practitioners consider that environments have the potential to create risky or protective climates.	Perspective-Taking Individuation
ACTIVITY 2.6: *My First Racial Memory*	Have practitioners consider the initial memories they have about race and ethnicity, and how those memories provide the framing for their current thinking.	Perspective-Taking Individuation Intergroup Contact
ACTIVITY 2.7: *Seeing Your Race-Life Journey*	Allow practitioners to discuss the racial and ethnic composition of personal friendships they have developed over their life journey.	Perspective-Taking Individuation Intergroup Contact
ACTIVITY 2.8: *Diversity Tables*	Provide practitioners the opportunity to explore the various dimensions of social identities, including individuals knowing the diversity of their own identities.	Perspective-Taking Individuation Intergroup Contact
ACTIVITY 2.9.1: *Replacing Colorblindness Statements*	Have practitioners closely examine colorblindness statements, identify how the statements are problematic, and develop replacement statements.	Perspective-Taking Individuation Intergroup Contact Improved Decision-Making
ACTIVITY 2.9.2: *Unpacking the Colorblindness Elephant—Survey Activity*	Using a survey activity, provide practitioners an opportunity to consider how colorblindness as an ideology relies on consistently framing or universalizing culture and minimizing differences of culture and identity.	Perspective-Taking Individuation Intergroup Contact
ACTIVITY 2.10: *Promoting Cultural Responsibility Beliefs*	Have practitioners closely examine cultural responsibility belief statements, identify how the statements are affirmative, and develop understanding of personal and professional work necessary to embody these statements.	Perspective-Taking Individuation Intergroup Contact
ACTIVITY 3.1: *Inventory of Friendship-Based Intercultural Interactions*	Have practitioners consider the level of individuation they are able to attain with their current friendship network. Activity: *Practitioners journal the type of friendship-based intercultural interactions they experience over an average week (seven days). The inventory should include the social identity of individuals and the premise of the friendship (i.e., How did the friendship emerge? Kids attend similar schools, colleagues work together, students attend same college, etc.).*	Perspective-Taking Individuation Intergroup Contact

APPENDIX 7. ADDITIONAL CROSS-CULTURAL ACTIVITIES

ACTIVITY	PURPOSE	PROMINENT INTERRUPTION STRATEGY
ACTIVITY 3.2: *Book Study for Racial, Ethnic, and Gender Expression–Based Perspective-Taking*	Have practitioners consider the type of books they are ready to explore for social identities differing from their own.	Perspective-Taking Individuation
Application Activity 1	Provide practitioners an opportunity to determine whether current book selections affirm racial, ethnic, and gender expression of students' identities.	Improved Decision-Making
Application Activity 2	Provide practitioners an opportunity to determine whether their current classrooms affirm racial, ethnic, and gender expression of students' identities.	Improved Decision-Making
Application Activity 3	Encourage practitioners to consider inserting demographic criteria into various practices in order to rehearse shifting into culture consciousness and identity affirmation beliefs.	Improved Decision-Making
Application Activity 4	Have practitioners apply culture consciousness and identity affirmation beliefs alongside various instructional and behavior-based books.	Improved Decision-Making

Appendix 8
Professional Development Template for Equity Belief Work

School Equity Team Tool

Purpose: To provide guidance on the development of a yearlong professional development sequence that considers the type of change (i.e., knowledge, attitude, skill, aspiration, or behavior) and the strategy (i.e., counter-stereotypic, improved decision-making, individuation, intergroup contact, or perspective-taking) for achieving that equity belief.

Type of Change: Professional development can have various desired outcomes or types of change. The following are various terms referenced in the template that relate to different types of change (Killion, 2008):

- **Knowledge:** conceptual understanding of information, theories, principles, and research
- **Attitude:** beliefs about the value of particular information or strategies
- **Skill:** ability to use strategies and processes to apply knowledge
- **Aspiration:** desire, or internal motivation, to engage in a particular practice
- **Behavior:** consistent application of knowledge and skills

APPENDIX 8. PROFESSIONAL DEVELOPMENT TEMPLATE FOR EQUITY BELIEF WORK

Process: This template is intended to assist in the outlining of a professional development for practitioners. The following are several steps to conduct before completing the template:

1. Decide on a theme for the year.
2. Consider the types of learners involved in the professional development. For example, does your staff enjoy reflection activities, hands-on activities, videos, readings, or other activities? Make sure to have a mix of learning activities that will reinforce the type of change that is expected.

Review the documents with readings, videos, and activities on race, identity, and cultural responsiveness in order to select the types of content that connect with the theme of the professional development (Fergus, 2016a, pp. 167–234).

MONTH	TYPE OF CHANGE: *KNOWLEDGE, ATTITUDE, SKILL, ASPIRATION, OR BEHAVIOR*	ACTIVITY	RESOURCES	APPLICATION (IF APPLICABLE): *WHAT YOU EXPECT THEM TO DO AS AN APPLICATION ACTIVITY*
September				
October				
November				

APPENDIX 8. PROFESSIONAL DEVELOPMENT TEMPLATE FOR EQUITY BELIEF WORK 147

MONTH	TYPE OF CHANGE: *KNOWLEDGE, ATTITUDE, SKILL, ASPIRATION, OR BEHAVIOR*	ACTIVITY/ STRATEGY	RESOURCES	APPLICATION (IF APPLICABLE): *WHAT YOU EXPECT THEM TO DO AS AN APPLICATION ACTIVITY*
December				
January				
February				

(Continued)

(Continued)

MONTH	TYPE OF CHANGE: *KNOWLEDGE, ATTITUDE, SKILL, ASPIRATION, OR BEHAVIOR*	ACTIVITY	RESOURCES	APPLICATION (IF APPLICABLE): *WHAT YOU EXPECT THEM TO DO AS AN APPLICATION ACTIVITY*
March				
April				
May				

References

Akil, M. B. (Creator). (2000–2008). *Girlfriends* [TV series]. Paramount Network Television; CBS Paramount Network Television; Grammnet Productions; Happy Camper Productions.

Alexander, E. C. (2018). Don't know or won't say? Exploring how colorblind norms shape item nonresponse in social surveys. *Sociology of Race and Ethnicity, 4*(3), 417–433. https://doi.org/10.1177/2332649217705145

Allport, G. W. (1954). *The nature of prejudice*. Addison-Wesley.

Allport, G. W. (1968). *The person in psychology*. Beacon Press.

Anda, R. F., Brown, D. W., Dube, S. R., Bremner, J. D., Felitti, V. J., & Giles, W. H. (2008). Adverse childhood experiences and chronic obstructive pulmonary disease in adults. *American Journal of Preventive Medicine, 34*(5), 396–403.

Anderson, C. (2016). *White rage*. Bloomsbury.

Apfelbaum, E. P., Sommers, S. R., & Norton, M. I. (2008). Seeing race and seeming racist? Evaluating strategic colorblindness in social interaction. *Journal of Personality and Social Psychology, 95*(4), 918–932. https://doi.org/10.1037/a0011990

Bandura, A. (1977). *Social learning theory*. Prentice Hall.

Bandura, A. (1986). *Social foundations of thought and action: A social-cognitive theory*. Prentice Hall.

Bandura, A. (1991). Social cognitive theory of self-regulation. *Organizational Behavior and Human Decision Processes, 50*, 248–287.

Banks, C. J., & Boulware, B. (Creators). (1985–1990). *227* [TV series]. Embassy Television; Embassy Communications; ELP Communications; Columbia Pictures Television.

Bell, D. (1992). *Faces at the bottom of the well: The permanence of racism*. Basic Books.

Bell, M. (2021). *Whiteness interrupted: White teachers and racial identity in predominantly Black schools*. Duke University Press.

Benton, R. (Writer & Director). (1979). *Kramer v. Kramer* [Film]. Columbia Pictures.

Bertrand, M., & Mullainathan, S. (2004). Are Emily and Greg more employable than Lakisha and Jamal? A field experiment on labor market discrimination. *American Economic Review, 94*(4), 991–1013.

Bickley, W., & Warren, M. (Creators). (1989–1998). *Family matters* [TV series]. Miller-Boyett Productions; Bickley-Warren Productions; Lorimar Television; Warner Bros. Television.

Black, S. E., Grönqvist, E., & Öckert, B. (2018). Born to lead? The effect of birth order on noncognitive abilities. *The Review of Economics and Statistics, 100*(2), 274–286. https://doi.org/10.1162/REST_a_00690

Blair, I. V., Ma, J. E., & Lenton, A. P. (2001). Imagining stereotypes away: The moderation of implicit stereotypes through mental imagery. *Journal of Personality and Social Psychology, 81*(5), 828–841. https://psycnet.apa.org/doi/10.1037/0022-3514.81.5.828

Blaisdell, B. (2005). Seeing every student as a 10: Using critical race theory to engage White teachers' colorblindness. *International Journal of Educational Policy, Research & Practice, 6*(1), 31–50.

Blanton, C. (2003). From intellectual deficiency to cultural deficiency: Mexican Americans, testing, and public school policy in the American Southwest, 1920–1940. *Pacific Historical Review, 72*(1), 39–62.

Bloom, B., Davis, A., & Hess, R. (1965). *Compensatory education for cultural deprivation*. Holt, Rinehart, and Winston.

Bobo, L. D., Charles, C. Z., Krysan, M., & Simmons, A. D. (2012). The *real* record on racial attitudes. In P. V. Marsden (Ed.), *Social trends in American life: Findings from the general social survey since 1972* (pp. 38–83). Princeton University Press.

Bodenhausen, G. V., Todd, A. R., & Richeson J. A. (2009). Controlling prejudice and stereotyping: Antecedents, mechanisms, and contexts. In T. D. Nelson (Ed.), *Handbook of prejudice, stereotyping, and discrimination* (pp. 111–135). Psychology Press.

Bonilla-Silva, E. (2006). *Racism without racists: Color-blind racism and persistence of racial inequality in America*. Rowman & Littlefield.

Bonilla-Silva, E. (2012). The invisible weight of Whiteness: The racial grammar of everyday life in America. *Michigan Sociological Review, 26*, 1–15.

Boutte, G., Lopez-Robertson, J., & Powers-Costello, E. (2011). Moving beyond color-blindness in early childhood classrooms. *Early Childhood Education Journal, 39*(5), 335–342. https://doi.org/10.1007/s10643-011-0457-x

Bowman, J., Lawrence, M., & Carew, T. (Creators). (1992–1997). *Martin* [TV series]. You Go Boy! Productions; HBO Independent Productions.

Bowser, Y. L. (Creator). (1993–1998). *Living single* [TV series]. SisterLee Productions; Warner Bros. Television.

Bradley, D. T., & Rice, A. L. (Creators). (1974–1975). *That's my mama* [TV series]. Blye-Beard Productions; Pollock/Davis, Inc.; Columbia Pictures.

Carter, P. L., Skiba, R., Arredondo, M. I., & Pollock, M. (2016). You can't fix what you don't look at: Acknowledging race in addressing racial discipline disparities. *Urban Education, 52*(2), 207–235. https://doi.org/10.1177/0042085916660350

Chinn, P. C., & Hughes, S. (1987). Representation of minority students in special education classes. *Remedial and Special Education, 8*(4), 41–46. https://doi.org/10.1177/074193258700800406

Chiu, C.-Y., Lonner, W. J., Matsumoto, D., & Ward, C. (2013). Cross-cultural competence: Theory, research, and application. *Journal of Cross-Cultural Psychology, 44*(6), 843–848. https://doi.org/10.1177/0022022113493716

Clark, K. B., & Clark, M. P. (1947). Racial identification and preference in Negro children. In T. M. Newcomb & E. L. Hartley (Eds.), *Readings in social psychology* (pp. 602–611). Holt, Rinehart & Winston.

Conwill, K., & Gardullo, P. (Eds.). (2021). *Make good promises: Reclaiming reconstruction and its legacies*. National Museum of African American History and Culture.

Cosby, W. H., Jr. (Creator). (1987–1993). *A different world* [TV series]. Carsey-Werner Productions in association with Bill Cosby.

Cosby, B., Weinberger, E., & Leeson, M. J. (Creators). (1984–1992). *The Cosby show* [TV series]. Carsey-Werner Productions in association with Bill Cosby.

Curry, T. J., & Curry, G. (2018), On the perils of race neutrality and anti-blackness: Philosophy as an irreconcilable obstacle to (Black) thought. *American Journal of Economics and Sociology, 77*, 657–687. https://doi.org/10.1111/ajes.12244

DiAngelo, R. (2018). *White fragility: Why it's so hard for White people to talk about racism*. Beacon Press.

DiTomaso, N., Parks-Yancy, R., & Post, C. (2003). White views of civil rights: Color blindness and equal opportunity. In A. W. Doane & E. Bonilla-Silva (Eds.), *White out: The continuing significance of racism* (1st ed., pp. 189–198). Routledge. https://doi.org/10.4324/9780203412107

Doane, A. W., & Bonilla-Silva, E. (Eds.). (2003). *White out: The continuing significance of racism*. Routledge.

Donato, R., & Hanson, J. S. (2012). Legally white, socially "Mexican": The politics of de jure and de facto school segregation in the American Southwest. *Harvard Educational Review, 82*(2), 202–225, 325–326.

Donnor, J. (2021). White fear, White flight, the rules of racial standing and Whiteness as property: Why two critical race theory constructs are better than one. *Educational Policy, 35*(2), 259–273.

Donovan, M. S., & Cross, C. T. (2002). *Minority students in special and gifted education.* National Academies Press. https://doi.org/10.17226/10128

Duckworth, A. L., Peterson, C., Matthews, M. D., & Kelly, D. R. (2007). Grit: Perseverance and passion for long-term goals. *Journal of Personality and Social Psychology, 92*(6), 1087–1101. https://doi.org/10.1037/0022-3514.92.6.1087

Dunn, L. M. (1968). Special education for the mildly retarded—is much of it justifiable? *Exceptional Children, 35*(1), 5–22.

DuRocher, K. (2011). *Raising racists: The socialization of white children in the Jim Crow South.* University Press of Kentucky.

Eberhardt, J. L., Goff, P. A., Purdie, V. J., & Davies, P. G. (2004). Seeing Black: Race, crime, and visual processing. *Journal of Personality and Social Psychology, 87*(6), 876–893.

Eitzen, M. B., & Baca-Zinn, D. S. (1994). *Social problems.* Allyn & Bacon.

Farquhar, R., Finney, S. V., & Spears, V. (Creators). (1996–2001). *Moesha* [TV series]. Regan Jon Productions; Seradipity Productions; Jump at the Sun Productions; Big Ticket Television.

Farrington, C. A., Roderick, M., Allensworth, E., Nagaoka, J., Keyes, T. S., Johnson, D. W., & Beechum, N. O. (2012). *Teaching adolescents to become learners. The role of noncognitive factors in shaping school performance: A critical literature review.* University of Chicago Consortium on Chicago School Research.

Felitti, V. J., Anda, R. F., Nordenberg, D., Williamson, D. F., Spitz, A. M., Edwards, V., Koss, M. P., & Marks, J. S. (1998). Relationship of childhood abuse and household dysfunction to many of the leading causes of death in adults: The Adverse Childhood Experiences (ACE) study. *American Journal of Preventive Medicine, 14*(4), 245–258. https://doi.org/10.1016/s0749-3797(98)00017-8

Fergus, E. (2004). *Skin color and identity formation: Perceptions of opportunity and academic orientation among Mexican and Puerto Rican youth.* Routledge.

Fergus, E. (2016a). *Solving disproportionality and achieving equity: A leader's guide to using data to change hearts and minds.* Corwin.

Fergus, E. (2016b). Social reproduction ideologies: Teacher beliefs about race and culture. In D. Connor, B. Ferri, & S. Annamma (Eds.), *DisCrit: Disability studies and critical race theory* (pp. 117–127). Teachers College Press.

Fergus, E., Noguera, P., & Martin, M. (2014). *Schooling for resilience: Improving the life trajectory of Black and Latino boys.* Harvard Education Press.

Fishbein, A., & Bunce, H. (2001). Subprime market growth and predatory lending. In S. M. Wachter & R. L. Penne (Eds.), *Housing policy in the new millennium: Conference proceedings* (pp. 273–288). U.S. Department of Housing and Urban Development.

Fiske, S. (1998). Stereotyping, prejudice, and discrimination. In S. Fiske, D. Gilbert, & L. Gardner (Eds.), *The handbook of social psychology* (pp. 357–411). McGraw-Hill.

Forman, T. A. (2004). Color-blind racism and racial indifference: The role of racial apathy in facilitating enduring inequalities. In M. Krysan & A. E. Lewis (Eds.), *The changing terrain of race and ethnicity* (pp. 43–66). Russell Sage.

Frankenberg, R. (1993). *White women, race matters.* Minnesota University Press.

Friedman, J., & Johnson, N. F. (2022, April). *Banned in the USA: Rising school book bans threaten free expression and students' First Amendment rights.* PEN America. https://pen.org/banned-in-the-usa/

Galinsky, A. D., & Moskowitz, G. B. (2000). Perspective-taking: Decreasing stereotype expression, stereotype accessibility, and in-group favoritism. *Journal of Personality and Social Psychology, 78*(4), 708–724. https://psycnet.apa.org/doi/10.1037/0022-3514.78.4.708

Galton, F. (1869). *Hereditary genius*. Macmillan.

Galton, F. (1904). Eugenics: Its definition, scope and aims. *The Sociological Review, sp1*(1), 43–51. https://doi.org/10.1177/0038026104SP100104

García, D. (2018). *Strategies of segregation: Race, residence, and the struggle for educational equality*. University of California Press.

García, O., & Torres-Guevara, R. (2009). Monoglossic ideologies and language policies in the education of U.S. Latinas/os. In J. Sánchez Muñoz, M. Machado-Casas, & E. G. Murillo, Jr. (Eds.), *Handbook of Latinos and education* (pp. 182–193). Routledge. https://doi.org/10.4324/9780203866078

Gilliam, W., Maupin, A., Reyes, C., Accavitti, M., & Shic, F. (2016). *Do early educators' implicit biases regarding sex and race relate to behavior expectations and recommendations for preschool expulsion and suspensions?* (Research Study Brief). Yale Child Study Center.

Gordon, J. (2005). Inadvertent complicity: Colorblindness in teacher education. *Educational Studies, 38*(2), 135–153.

Grossman, J. (2016, August 3). James Baldwin on history. *AHA Today*. https://www.historians.org/research-and-publications/perspectives-on-history/summer-2016/james-baldwin-on-history

Haley, A. (Writer). (1977). *Roots: The saga of an American family* [TV miniseries]. Wolper Productions.

Harris, C. I. (1993). Whiteness as property. *Harvard Law Review, 106*(8), 1707–1791.

Harris, S. (Creator). (1979–1986). *Benson* [TV series]. Witt/Thomas/Harris Productions.

Hart, B., & Risley, T. R. (1995). *Meaningful differences in the everyday experience of young American children*. P. H. Brookes.

Hartmann, D., Croll, P. R., Larson, R., Gerteis, J., & Manning, A. (2017). Colorblindness as identity: Key determinants, relations to ideology, and implications for attitudes about race and policy. *Sociological Perspectives, 60*(5), 866–888. https://doi.org/10.1177/0731121417719694

Helford, B., Lopez, G., & Borden, R. (Creators). (2002–2007). *George Lopez* [TV series]. Fortis Productions; Mohawk Productions; Warner Bros. Television.

Heller, C. (1966). *Mexican American youth: The forgotten youth at the crossroads*. Random House.

Hollingworth, L. S. (1926). *Gifted children: Their nature and nurture*. Macmillan.

Horta, S. (Developer). (2006–2010). *Ugly Betty* [TV series]. Ventanarosa Productions; Silent H Productions; Reveille Productions; ABC Studios.

Ignatiev, N. (2009). *How the Irish became White*. Routledge Press.

Johnson, H. B., & Shapiro, T. M. (2003). Good neighborhoods, good schools: Race and the "good choices" of White families. In A. W. Doane & E. Bonilla-Silva (Eds.), *White out: The continuing significance of racism* (pp. 173–187). Routledge.

Jost, J. T., & Hunyady, O. (2005). Antecedents and consequences of system-justifying ideologies. *Current Directions in Psychological Science, 14*(5), 260–265. http://www.jstor.org/stable/20183040

Khan, N. (Creator). (2015–2020). *Fresh off the boat* [TV series]. Fierce Baby Productions; The Detective Agency; 20th Century Fox Television.

Killion, J. (2008). *Assessing impact: Evaluating staff development*. Corwin.

Komack, J. (Creator). (1974–1978). *Chico and the man* [TV series]. The Komack Company Inc.; Wolper Productions.

Lachman, M., & Rosen, S. (Creators). (1981–1987). *Gimme a break!* [TV series]. Mort Lachman and Associates; Alan Landsburg Productions; Reeves Entertainment Group; MCA TV.

Ladson-Billings, G. (1994). *The dreamkeepers: Successful teachers of African American children*. Jossey-Bass.

Lasater, K., Bengston, E., & Albiladi, W. (2021). Data use for equity?: How data practices incite deficit thinking in schools. *Studies in Educational Evaluation, 69*, 100845.

Lawton, J. F. (Writer), & Marshall, G. (Director). (1990). *Pretty woman* [Film]. Touchstone

Pictures; Silver Screen Partners IV; Regency International Pictures.

Lee, H. (1960). *To kill a mockingbird*. Lippincott.

Lee, S. (Writer, Director, & Producer). (1989). *Do the right thing* [Film]. 40 Acres and a Mule Filmworks.

Lewis, O. (1961). *The children of Sanchez*. Random House.

Levy, S. (2016). Parents', students', and teachers' beliefs about teaching heritage histories in public school history classrooms. *Journal of Social Studies Research, 40*(1), 5–20.

Lonner, W. J. (2014). Cross cultural. In K. D. Keith (Ed.), *The encyclopedia of cross-cultural psychology*. Wiley.

Manning, A., Hartmann, D., & Gerteis, J. (2015). Colorblindness in Black and White: An analysis of core tenets, configurations, and complexities. *Sociology of Race & Ethnicity, 1*(4), 532.

McNeill, L. (2017, October 26). How a psychologist's work on race identity helped overturn school segregation in 1950s America. *Smithsonian Magazine*. https://www.smithsonianmag.com/science-nature/psychologist-work-racial-identity-helped-overturn-school-segregation-180966934/

Meeussen, L., Otten, S., & Phalet, K. (2014). Managing diversity: How leaders' multiculturalism and colorblindness affect work group functioning. *Group Processes & Intergroup Relations, 17*(5), 629–644.

Miller, A. (1949). *Death of a salesman*. Viking Press.

Molenberghs, P., & Louis, W. R. (2018). Insights from fMRI studies into ingroup bias. *Frontiers in Psychology, 9*, 1868. https://doi.org/10.3389/fpsyg.2018.01868

Monte, E. (Creator). (1976–1979). *What's happening!!* [TV series]. Bud Yorkin Productions; TOY Productions.

Monte, E., & Evans, M. (Creators). (1974–1979). *Good times* [TV series]. Tandem Productions.

Muhammad, G. (2017). *Cultivating genius: An equity framework for culturally and historically responsive literacy*. Scholastic.

Nicholl, D., Ross, M., & West, B. (Creators). (1975–1985). *The Jeffersons* [TV series]. T.A.T. Communications Company; NRW Productions; Ragamuffin Productions; Embassy Television.

Oakes, J. (1985). *Keeping track: How schools structure inequality*. Yale University Press.

O'Connor, C., & Fernandez, S. D. (2006). Race, class, and disproportionality: Reevaluating the relationship between poverty and special education placement. *Educational Researcher, 35*(6), 6–11.

O'Donnell, P. (2020). When code words aren't coded. *Social Theory & Practice, 46*(4), 813–845.

Oh, E., Choi, C. C., Neville, H. A., Anderson, C. J., Landrum-Brown, J. (2010). Beliefs about affirmative action: A test of the group self-interest and racism beliefs models. *Journal of Diversity in Higher Education, 3*, 163.

Ondrich, J., Ross, S., & Yinger, J. (2003). Now you see it, now you don't: Why do real estate agents withhold available houses from Black customers? *Review of Economics and Statistics, 85*(4), 854–873.

Oswald, M. E., & Grosjean, S. (2004). Confirmation bias. In R. F. Pohl (Ed.), *Cognitive illusions: A handbook on fallacies and biases in thinking, judgement and memory* (pp. 79–96). Psychology Press.

Pager, D., Bonikowski, B., & Western, B. (2009). Discrimination in a low-wage labor market: A field experiment. *American Sociological Review, 74*(5), 777–799. https://doi.org/10.1177/000312240907400505

Perry, T. (Creator). (2006–2023). *Tyler Perry's house of Payne* [TV series]. Tyler Perry Studios; Georgia Media; SAG-AFTRA; BET Original Productions.

Pettigrew, T. F. (1998). Intergroup contact theory. *Annual Review of Psychology, 49*, 65–85.

Pettigrew, T. F., & Tropp, L. R. (2006). A meta-analytic test of intergroup contact theory. *Journal of Personality and Social Psychology, 90*, 751–783.

Public Religion Research Institute. (2022, May 24). *American bubbles: Politics, race, and religion in Americans' core friendship networks.* https://www.prri.org/research/american-bubbles-politics-race-and-religion-in-americans-core-friendship-networks/

Puzo, M. (Writer), & Coppola, F. F. (Writer & Director). (1972). *The godfather* [Film]. Paramount Pictures; Alfran Productions.

Rasmussen, L., & Sieck, W. (2015). Culture-general competence: Evidence from a cognitive field study of professionals who work in many cultures. *International Journal of Intercultural Relations, 48*, 75–90.

Reo, D., & Wayans, D. (Creators). (2001–2005). *My wife and kids* [TV series]. Wayans Bros. Entertainment; Impact Zone Productions; Touchstone Television.

Silver, S. (Creator). (1983–1989). *Webster* [TV series]. Georgian Bay Ltd.; Emmanuel Lewis Entertainment Enterprises; Paramount Network Television; Paramount Domestic Television.

Singleton, J. (Writer & Director). (1991). *Boyz n the hood* [Film]. Columbia Pictures.

Skiba, R. J., Michael, R. S., Nardo, A. C., & Peterson, R. L. (2002). The color of discipline: Sources of racial and gender disproportionality in school punishment. *The Urban Review, 34*, 317–342.

Small, M. L., Harding D., & Lamont M. (2010). Introduction: Reconsidering culture and poverty. *The Annals of the American Academy of Political and Social Science, 629*, 6–27.

Soss, J., Fording, R., & Schram, S. (2011). *Disciplining the poor: Neoliberal paternalism and the persistent power of race.* University of Chicago Press.

Soss, J., & Weaver, V. (2016). Learning from Ferguson: Welfare, criminal justice, and the political science of race and class. In J. Hooker & A. B. Tillery Jr. (Eds.), *The double bind: The politics of racial and class inequalities in the Americas, a report of the task force on racial and social class.* American Political Science Association. https://www.apsanet.org/Portals/54/files/Task%20Force%20Reports/Hero%20Report%202016_The%20Double%20Bind/7_Soss%20and%20Weaver.pdf

Spencer, M. B. (2006). Phenomenology and ecological systems theory: Development of diverse groups. In W. Damon & R. M. Lerner (Series Eds.), & R. M. Lerner (Vol. Ed.), *Handbook of child psychology: Vol. 1. Theoretical models of human development* (6th ed., pp. 829–893). John Wiley.

Sperry, D., Sperry, L., & Miller, P. (2018). Reexamining the verbal environments of children from different socioeconomic backgrounds. *Child Development, 90*(4), 1303–1318. https://doi.org/10.1111/cdev.13072

Taylor et al. (2019).

Terman, L. M. (1916). *The measurement of intelligence: An explanation of and a complete guide for the use of the Stanford revision and extension of the Binet-Simon scales.* Houghton Mifflin.

Terman, L. M. (1925). *Genetic studies of genius. Mental and physical traits of a thousand gifted children.* Stanford University Press.

Thomas, A. (2017). *The hate u give.* Balzer & Bray.

Twain, M. (1885). *Adventures of Huckleberry Finn (Tom Sawyer's comrade).* Webster.

U.S. Government Accountability Office. (2022, June). *Student population has significantly diversified, but many schools remain divided along racial, ethnic, and economic lines* (Report No. GAO-22-104737). https://www.gao.gov/assets/gao-22-104737.pdf

Valencia, R. R. (1997). *The evolution of deficit thinking: Educational thought and practice.* Falmer Press.

van der Zee, K. I., & van Oudenhoven, J. P. (2000). The multicultural personality questionnaire: A multidimensional instrument of multicultural effectiveness. *European Journal of Personality, 14*(4), 291–309. https://doi.org/10.1002/1099-0984(200007/08)14:4<291::AID-PER377>3.0.CO;2-6

Wayans, K. I. (Creator). (1990–1994). *In living color* [TV series]. Ivory Way Productions; 20th Century Fox Television; 20th Television.

Weinberger, E. (Creator). (1986–1991). *Amen* [TV series]. Carson Productions; Stein & Illes Productions.

Wilmore, L. (Creator). (2001–2006). *The Bernie Mac show* [TV series]. Wilmore Films; Regency Television; 20th Century Fox Television.

Wilson, E. K. (2021). Monopolizing Whiteness. *Harvard Law Review*, *134*(7). https://harvardlawreview.org/print/vol-134/monopolizing-whiteness/

Wilson, F. (Host). (1970–1974). *The Flip Wilson show* [TV series]. NBC.

Wilson, J., Ward, C., & Fischer, R. (2013). Beyond culture learning theory: What can personality tell us about cultural competence? *Journal of Cross-Cultural Psychology*, *44*(6), 900–927.

Wilt, C. L., Annamma, S. A., Wilmot, J. M., Nyegenye, S. N., Miller, A. L., & Jackson, E. E. (2022). Performing color-evasiveness: A DisCrit analysis of educators' discourse in the U.S. *Teaching and Teacher Education*, *117*, 103761.

Wing Sue, D. (2016). *Race talk and the conspiracy of silence*. Wiley.

Yorkin, B., & Lear, N. (Executive Producers). (1972–1977). *Sanford & son* [TV series]. NBC.

Index

abilities and behaviors, 141
academic performance, 56–57, 91, 97
ACE (Adverse Childhood Experiences), 149, 151
activities, reflection, 132, 136, 145
Advanced Placement. *See* AP
Adverse Childhood Experiences (ACE), 149, 151
affinity and associational biases, 12, 14, 22, 49–50, 116
affinity bias, 12–13, 39, 85, 94, 108
African Americans, 21–22, 30, 45, 49, 64, 88, 152
age, 9, 13, 27, 52, 74, 131, 135
agreements, 37, 55, 80
Allport, G. W., 47, 115, 117, 149
AP (Advanced Placement), 7, 16, 37, 44, 48, 56, 59, 76, 84, 98
application, 101, 146–48, 150
Asian communities, 55, 84
Asian cultures, 84
Asian students, 5, 16, 44, 48, 84, 86, 109, 118
aspiration, 144, 146–48
assumptions, 1–2, 9, 14, 41, 83, 96, 98, 102, 112
athletics, 5–6
attire, 100
attitudes, 1, 17, 120–21, 144, 146–48, 152
   racial, 52, 74, 150
attributes, 16–17, 92, 104
   cultural, 88, 93
authorities, 101, 117–19

Bandura, A., 57, 149
behaviors
   individual, 82, 105–6, 115
   suspicious, 15
   universal, 141
behaviors for success, 141
beliefs, system-justifying, 82
Benjamin Franklin High School, 100
bias-based beliefs, addressing, 132, 136
biases, 3, 7–8, 13, 17, 74, 85, 98, 112, 117, 153

BIPOC students, 7, 11
Black and Latinx students in special education, 68
Black parents, 31, 84
Black students, overrepresentation of, 71, 95, 111
BMI (body mass index), 50
boarding schools, 24–25
body mass index (BMI), 50
Bonilla-Silva, E. 69–70, 150, 152
brainstorm, 108, 133, 137
Brown, 3, 7, 10, 17, 30, 33, 60, 75–76, 121, 149
Brown students, 8–9, 50, 59

California, 25–26, 28, 93
camps, 22, 24
Carlisle Indian School, 25
case studies, 28–29
cause, 54, 75, 92, 96
Census, 26–28, 77
Census Bureau, 4, 26, 28
change, 68, 110, 144–48
colorblind, 72, 83
colorblind identification, 83
colorblindness ideology, 72, 76, 83–84, 89, 120
colorblind perspective, 72
color-evasiveness, 72–73, 84
common goals, 117–18
communities
   low-income, 98–99, 102
   suburb, 40
competence, cross-cultural, 120–21, 150
competencies, 121–22, 127, 138
Congress, 25, 44, 51
contact theory, 116–17
   intergroup, 153
Cosby, W. H., 68, 150
cost, 76, 82, 110–11
counter-stereotypic imaging, 123
crimes, 22, 40, 73, 92, 151

157

critical race theory, 40, 62, 117, 149, 151
cross-cultural experiences, 9, 12, 38, 45, 49, 52
   absence of, 76, 87
cross-cultural knowledge and skills, 18, 65, 120
cultural deficiency, 93, 97–98, 102, 149
cultural empathy, 120–21
cultural experiences, 3, 9–10, 89
cultural features, 22, 25, 29, 91
cultural groups, 79, 85, 124
cultural knowledge, 115, 122, 128
cultural practices, 97, 101–2
cultural references, 79, 86
curriculum, national, 55
Curry, T. J., 75, 150

deaths, 75, 151, 153
decision, 2–3, 33, 54
Defenders of State Sovereignty and Individual Liberties, 33
deficit orientation, 106, 109, 141
deficits, cultural, 84, 96, 98
deficit thinking and poverty disciplining, 89, 91–92, 106, 113, 136
deficit thinking ideology, 91–92, 141
devaluation, 4–5, 18, 54–55, 91
diminishment, cultural, 120
diplomatic mindset, 121, 123–25, 139
discipline, 7, 40–41, 84, 92, 98–99, 101, 154
discipline practices, 118
dispositions, 18, 49, 58, 76, 116, 120
disproportionality, 3, 7–8, 19, 48, 84, 117, 153
disproportionate pattern of White and Asian students, 5, 16
disrespect, 13, 93–94, 98
district leadership, 69, 118–19
diversity, 34, 59, 64, 67, 116, 124–25, 142, 153
doll, 15, 53
domain, 121–22

EBT (Electronic Benefits Transfer), 14
economic conditions, 47, 110
effect, detrimental, 2–3
Electronic Benefits Transfer (EBT), 14
emancipation, 54–55
enrollment, 7, 38–39, 98, 112
   public school, 38, 40
   student school, 38
enrollment of students in special education, 112
environmental factors, 16, 111

environments, 119, 122–23, 125, 142
equal group status, 117
equal status, 117, 119
equity, educational, 3, 31, 140
eugenics, 42, 44, 94–95, 152
evolution, cultural, 84
experiment, 52–53

fear, 18, 40, 45, 47, 51–52, 62, 64–65, 70, 81
fear language, 40, 62
fear of losing Whiteness, 55, 61–62
Ferguson, 2, 37, 154
focus groups, 76
framing, 29, 69, 95, 108, 118, 141–42
friendship groups, 19

Galton, F., 42, 94, 152
GAO (Government Accountability Office), 38–39, 154
García, O., 29, 152
gender, 9–11, 22, 64, 69, 73, 75, 117, 131
genesis, 18, 52–53, 93
ghetto, 85
gifted children, 43–44, 152, 154
gifted programs, 16, 40–41, 45, 85–86
gifted students, 41, 43
gifts, 8, 41, 43
government, 23–25, 112
Government Accountability Office. See GAO
Green Valley East School District, 101
grit, 17, 56–58, 91–92, 151
Guadalupe Hidalgo, 26, 28

Hartmann, D., 83, 152–53
health insurance, 111–12
Heller, C., 97, 152
Hispanic, 49, 74, 77, 88
history of Whiteness ideology, 44
Hollingworth, L. S., 42–43, 152
home, broken, 108
Honors, 16, 44, 56, 59, 76, 93, 97
Honors classes for Black students, 84
House Bill, 62, 64

identification, 129
   racial, 52, 77–78, 129
identities
   non-White, 4–5, 52
   social, 69–70, 132, 136, 142–43
identity affirmation beliefs, 143

Indigenous populations, 23, 26, 75–76, 121
individualism, 22, 79, 82–83, 110
individual liberties, 33–34
individuating, 123–24
inferiority, 2–3, 23, 29, 37
intercultural interaction, 121–25, 139
  friendship-based, 142
intergroup contact, 117, 123, 140–42, 144
intergroup experiences, 117–18, 121

language, coded, 16, 73, 76
Latinx student population, 48
Latinx students in special education, 68
legitimize, 83
letters, 34, 54, 99–101, 109–10
Lewis, O., 97, 151, 153
liberty, 34, 63, 79
losing Whiteness, 55, 61–62

MALDEF (Mexican American Legal Defense and Educational Fund), 55
marginalization, 70–71, 92, 125
marginalized groups, 56, 70, 125
meritocracy, 22, 56, 63, 82–83
Mexican American Legal Defense and Educational Fund (MALDEF), 55
Mexican Americans, 15, 21, 28, 30, 45, 64, 93, 149, 152
Mexicans, 18, 23, 26, 28–29, 32, 42, 126, 150
minoritized students, 12, 17
minority students, 79, 150–51
minority students in special education classes, 150
misbehaviors, understanding student, 121
models, 10, 84, 93
  genetic pathology, 92–93, 106
monkeys, 8, 87
monocultural experiences, 9–10, 49, 51

NAACP (National Association for the Advancement of Colored People), 3, 55
national anthem, 87
National Association for Gifted Children, 43
National Association for the Advancement of Colored People (NAACP), 3, 55
Native Americans, 15, 21, 23–25, 38–39, 41, 45, 48, 55, 126
noncognitive skills, 56
Norfolk Public Schools, 34
N-word, 49, 86, 88

Old Dominion University Libraries, 33–34, 36–37
orphanages, 109–10
orphans, 109–10
overrepresentation of BIPOC students in special education, 7
overrepresentation of Black students in special education, 95
overrepresentation of White and Asian students in gifted programs, 16

patterns, disproportionate, 108, 118
patterns of segregation, 39
perseverance, 56–58, 151
personality, 56, 149, 151, 153–55
perspective, 72–73, 111–12, 118, 121, 139
Pettigrew, T. F., 117, 123, 153
pillars, 3, 7
PLC (Professional Learning Community), 97, 118
policies and practices, 83
populations, minoritized, 9, 57–58, 74, 82, 92, 116
poverty, 40, 54, 82, 91–92, 96, 98–99, 102–3, 153–54
  culture of, 93, 97–98, 112
poverty disciplining beliefs, 98–99, 116, 121
poverty disciplining ideologies, 113
powerlines, 111
practices
  employment, 64, 70
  schools use, 95
Predominantly White Institution (PWI), 111
preference, 50, 52–53, 150
prejudgments, 115–17
prejudice, 73, 115–17, 149–51
preschool expulsions, 14, 152
presumption, 10, 17, 47, 79, 103, 105–6, 108–10, 112
process of school segregation, 25
professional development, 144–45
Professional Learning Community (PLC), 97, 118
purpose, 10, 30, 73–74, 140–44
PWI (Predominantly White Institution), 111

race
  child's, 78
  seeing, 78, 82, 149
race and racism, 74–75

racial differences, 53, 107
racial/ethnic minority students, 141
racist, 63, 73–74, 76, 86, 149–50
referrals
  behavioral, 16, 85, 125
  disciplinary, 7–8, 98–99
resources, hoarding of, 60
restroom, 112

sanction, 2–3, 60
schools and society, 7, 99
school segregation, 3, 10, 21, 25, 35, 38–39, 42, 54, 82
  patterns highlight, 39
school systems, 3, 25, 28, 44
  racial integrated, 3, 60
school values, 105
scientific racism, 53, 94–95
segregated schools, 2, 30, 33, 120
segregation, residential, 69
segregation of Mexican students, 37
self-assessment, 138–39
sex and race, 14, 152
sexist, 63
SGI (small group instruction), 109
Shelby County, 40
skills and attitudes, 121
slavery, 2, 21–22
social closure, 58–61
Soss, J., 99, 154
special education, 7, 37, 40–41, 68–69, 95, 102, 111–12, 150–51
special education identification, 84
speech, 54, 92
State Sovereignty and Individual Liberties, 33
stereotyping, 5, 150–51
strategy of segregating Native Americans in off-reservation boarding schools, 24
student enrollment, 36, 86
student population, 17, 54, 109, 154

students
  disadvantaged, 103
  female, 87, 112
  individual, 103
  low-income, 111
students in special education, 112
student teacher, 11
study of educator perceptions of race, 76
suburbs, 39
Supreme Court, 2–3, 55, 61, 113
survey activity, 141–42

talented education, 43–44
teacher education, 152, 155
template, 144–45
Tennessee, 31–32, 34, 40
Terman, L. M., 42–43, 154
themes, 65, 122, 145
toilet paper, 112
trauma, 102–3
treaty, 26, 28

valuation, 10, 30, 32, 55, 83
valuation of whiteness, 18, 34, 37, 54–55, 60–62, 83
videos, 14, 61, 70, 145
violence, 65, 96–97, 102, 116

Washington High School, Booker T., 36–37
White and Asian students in gifted programs, 86
White colonizers, 23
Whiteness-derived prejudgments, 116
Whiteness ideology in sustaining segregated schools, 40
White parents and educators, 61
Wilson, E. K., 31, 58, 68, 120, 155
Writer, 152–54

Yale Child Study Center, 14

CORWIN
A Sage Company

Helping educators make the greatest impact

CORWIN HAS ONE MISSION: to enhance education through intentional professional learning.

We build long-term relationships with our authors, educators, clients, and associations who partner with us to develop and continuously improve the best evidence-based practices that establish and support lifelong learning.